Smarter Clicking

SCHOOL TECHNOLOGY POLICIES THAT WORK!

Smarter Clicking

SCHOOL TECHNOLOGY POLICIES THAT WORK!

CHRISTOPHER WELLS

A Joint Publication

For information:

Corwin
A SAGE Company
2455 Teller Road
Thousand Oaks, California 91320
(800) 233-9936
Fax: (800) 417-2466
www.corwin.com

SAGE Ltd.
1 Oliver's Yard
55 City Road
London EC1Y 1SP
United Kingdom

SAGE India Pvt. Ltd.
B 1/I 1 Mohan Cooperative
    Industrial Area
Mathura Road,
    New Delhi 110 044
India

SAGE Asia-Pacific Pte. Ltd.
33 Pekin Street #02-01
Far East Square
Singapore 048763

Printed in the United States of America.

Library of Congress Cataloging-in-Publication Data

Wells, Christopher.
Smarter clicking : school technology policies that work! / Christopher Wells.
    p. cm.

"A Joint publication with the American Association of School Administrators and National Association of Secondary School Principals."

Includes bibliographical references and index.
ISBN 978-1-4129-6699-3 (pbk.)
    1. Educational technology—United States—Planning. I. Title.

LB1028.3.W4 2010
371.33--dc22   2009051388

This book is printed on acid-free paper.

10   11   12   13   14   10   9   8   7   6   5   4   3   2   1

Acquisitions Editor:	Debra Stollenwerk
Associate Editor:	Julie McNall
Production Editor:	Eric Garner
Copy Editor:	Tomara Kafka
Typesetter:	C&M Digitals (P) Ltd.
Proofreader:	Joyce Li
Indexer:	Wendy Allex
Cover Designer:	Michael Dubowe

Contents

Preface

We are stuck with technology when what we really want is just stuff that works.

—Douglas Adams (2002), *The Salmon of Doubt*

Beware the Four Horsemen of the Information Apocalypse: terrorists, drug dealers, kidnappers, and child pornographers. Seems like you can scare any public into allowing the government to do anything with those four.

—Bruce Scheier (2005), *Computer Crime Hype*

Technology has created a whole new realm of decision-making challenges, and as the quotes above indicate, technology is not the tame, managed tool that it was envisioned to be. Instead, technology is handheld and room-sized, invisibly available or connected with a wire, person to person or device to device. To make sense of our world, we create rules that are the basis of all policies and procedures. Technology policies and procedures often suffer from being too limiting or too nebulous, both of which are almost impossible to enforce. What do we as educators do to protect our students and staff members from the "four horsemen" that Bruce Scheier mentioned and still use technology to get the job of teaching and learning done, which is supported by Douglas Adams' quote?

RATIONALE

As a school district administrator for one of the largest school districts in the United States, I realized that the questions arriving on my desk were being heard around the country. Whether at conferences, through e-mail queries, during presentations, or written about in instructional technology publications, building useful—and effective—technology policies and procedures is a major source of concern for schools and districts.

This book is the result of my work with students, parents, teachers, and administrators as we struggled with the emergence of technology as an essential classroom resource. Just like desks, school buildings, and cafeterias, technology is no longer a luxury but has become an essential resource throughout schools and district offices. The regulation of technology must be a top priority with many districts, because students and teachers are finding ways to use technology that are not supporting the core business of teaching and learning. Creating solid, useful, and simple policies and procedures is a time-consuming process, and this book provides guidance to streamline the process and make the development of policies and procedures as simple as possible.

AUDIENCE AND APPROACH

Principals, administrators, and technology team members are the key audience for this book because these members of the school community either struggle with students and parents to enforce the rules and implement the policies. With this in hand, you will be able to construct instructional technology policies and procedures that are consistent with the school and district resources and supported by the school community.

For administrators, this text will prepare you for the immediate future of technology in your school. Considering the types of challenges that administrators already face with cell phones and student-developed Web pages, there are practical suggestions for keeping your school within legal guidelines and ethical boundaries. There are also many short, clear descriptions of the types of technology you might be implementing in your school. Another component that might make your job a little easier is a clear review of the legal implications of school technology use, especially when challenged by parents or staff members on their rights when using school equipment. I have included tips for protecting your technology investment and practical guidelines for implementing instructional technology policies and procedures in your school or district.

For technology team members, this book will provide leadership ideas to help you create a community of learning through technology, instead of an "electronic lockdown" where students and staff members feel restricted. As guardians of the school technology, your expanding role is essential to schools and districts, because your role allows teachers to connect rich resources to the learning process. This book's approach is to help you think through the policy development and implementation process thoroughly, avoiding costly pitfalls that jeopardize student and staff success. You can use this text to prepare for discussions around student data privacy, contribute the policy-making process, or communicate existing policies and procedures to the school community.

ORGANIZATION AND RESOURCES

This text is organized with an initial emphasis on the importance of school technology policies and then the cast of school characters who will be part of the policy development process. The following chapters present practical steps and resources on the fundamental topics being discussed in schools around the country. These topics include data privacy, investment protection, acceptable use policies (commonly referred to as AUPs), Internet use. A discussion on the implementation of school technology policies and procedures follows, and the book concludes with an optimistic look at emerging technology.

An additional Resources section of the text provides more specific guidance on some policies and procedures your school or district might need to develop or implement. AUPs, Internet access policies, and school Web page guidelines are presented in easy-to-follow outlines.

If you are reading this book with a specific emphasis in mind, this topical guideline might be useful:

Content Area	Ch 1	Ch 2	Ch 3	Ch 4	Ch 5	Ch 6	Ch 7	Ch 8
Why school technology policies are important	X	X		X				
Who should be involved in school technology policy development		X					X	
Who should be involved in school technology policy implementation							X	X
Protecting student data	X	X	X		X	X	X	X
Developing AUPs					X			
Defining the gaps in instructional technology policies and procedures	X		X	X	X			X
Describing the roles that technology team members play in policy activities		X	X	X	X	X	X	X

Another resource in this book that you may find useful are the critical chapter questions at the beginning of each chapter along with the chapter focus. If you are looking for specific content areas, these questions are consistent with the *essential* questions many teachers use to focus class lessons. These questions are also the specific areas of concern to many school districts around the country and might be useful when you are having discussions around technology policies and procedures in your own school or district.

Finally, it is important to know that a book like this may only serve to raise more questions. If nothing else, administrators and technology team members in schools and districts will be better prepared to answer the questions that are emerging throughout the world regarding computer use and technology management in the school setting. This text was never meant to answer all of the questions because so many of the answers depend on the readers' circumstances, such as school district positions, interactions with the school community, and funding levels for both school and district. Instead, the goal of writing a resource like this was to open the door to teaching and learning in a safer, more effective way through the appropriate use of technology. Much like Douglas Adams' sentiment, "stuff that works" in education should have a lasting impact for future generations, which is why discussions about the safe and wise use of technology for schools is so important.

Acknowledgments

Corwin gratefully acknowledges the contributions of the following individuals:

Laurie Emery
Principal
Old Vail Middle School
Vail, Arizona

Richard Jones
Middle School Principal
Rochester Public Schools
Rochester, Minnesota

Toni Jones
Director of Secondary Curriculum and Instructional Technology
Deer Creek Public Schools
Edmond, Oklahoma

Donnan Stoicovy
Elementary Principal
State College Area School District
Park Forest Elementary School
State College, Pennsylvania

About the Author

Christopher Wells is the IT policies and communications director for Gwinnett County Public Schools, the largest school district in Georgia. With more than 160,000 students in the district, he responds to the diverse, creative ways technology is being used in classrooms. Christopher presents regularly and his enthusiasm for his topic material is contagious (even if the audience thinks that technology policies and procedures are boring!). By incorporating realistic examples and messages with humor, compassion, and vision, Christopher consistently engages diverse audiences and leaves listeners focused and energized on the development of new resources for students and teachers. In the past, he worked for Arthur Andersen, a global consulting firm, and developed and managed a global distance learning consulting practice. Prior to that, Christopher was a high school science and computer science teacher, developing curricula for biology, ecology, environmental science, oceanography, science research, and AP Pascal classes.

Christopher is a graduate of the Florida Institute of Technology in Melbourne, Florida, earning his BS in science education and biology and an MS in computer education with an emphasis on instructional technology. He is currently a PhD student at Walden University's College of Management and Technology in leadership and organizational change. Christopher is still actively involved in several organizations that involve youth and the natural world, including a youth retreat movement for middle-school students and a sea turtle research project run on Wassaw Island, Georgia.

E-mail Christopher at cwells@schooltechpolicies.com or visit his Web site at www.schooltechpolicies.com.

Optional No Longer

The Need for Effective
School Technology Policies

Critical Chapter Questions

- What is the purpose for school technology policies?
- What do students, staff, and parents expect from school technology?
- Why are policies necessary for technology use?

Chapter Focus: *Define the value of school technology policies and proce-dures and the importance of policies for instruction.*

❖

Jacob has been an elementary school teacher for 15 years and works in a school between an affluent community and a farm community. The changes that have entered the classroom, as well as those that have left the classroom, have usually been positive, and Jacob looks at new "education fads" as opportunities to add one or two new ideas to his solid, and effective, teaching style. One of the more positive changes in his classroom in the last few years has been an influx of computers and educational software into the school. In fact, more and more professional learning opportunities are focused on specific tools for teaching and skill reinforcement, and Jacob has enjoyed working with other teachers to create lessons for his classroom. From conversations with other teachers in his district, Jacob knows that his school is about average, with several computer labs in addition to classroom computers, and many of the schools are using the same teaching and learning software. Jacob is keenly aware of the students' expectations to have more computer access and wonders how the middle and high schools are keeping up with the students' technology needs each year.

How is a computer used in a classroom? It's easy to imagine students and teachers sitting at computers and using them to read or send e-mails, type documents, and complete instructional assignments with specialized programs. It's a little more difficult to imagine a teacher or student using a classroom computer to purchase stocks and bonds during class time instead of teaching and learning, post locker-room pictures of students on a Web page, or capture standardized test items to gain "an edge" before a big test. Unfortunately, all of those situations are real—both students and teachers have done all of those things with the technology provided by schools or school districts like yours and mine.

WHY SCHOOL TECHNOLOGY POLICIES ARE ESSENTIAL

Consider a recent court case reported in *USA Today:* A middle school locker room was under camera surveillance. The cameras were noticed by a visiting sports team at a multischool event. During the investigation, it was found that the images of students undressing were even available through the Internet for remote surveillance (Associated Press News, 2007). Since an agent of the school was responsible for installing the cameras as part of a security initiative, the Overton School Board was charged as guilty of civil negligence and had to pay the affected students a settlement. While this may seem like an isolated incident, other school districts have worked to remove cameras from inappropriate locations and have written policies to prevent such events from happening at their schools.

School technology policies and procedures are the guidelines for appropriate technology use in the school environment. Policies shape the day-to-day use of school technology, define boundaries around student and staff member behaviors, and clarify technology use issues and concerns for parents and community members. Designed and implemented properly, policies become living documents that can weave a community around the infusion of technology into schools and school districts as well as protect students and the school. For clarity, let's define the terms *policy* and *procedure* as well as consider what might fall into the category of *local* school policies and procedures.

Policy

Policies are usually short, single-topic documents to establish the school board position on a specific topic of education. A policy is passed by the school board and usually reviewed by the board's legal counsel. As a public document, a policy is openly available, and many school districts post their official and approved policies on districts' Web pages. Many policies include standard statements as quasi-governmental agencies, such as nondiscrimination statements or organizational documents. In some cases, specific policy areas are required by the state or federal departments of education to align schools with state or national standards.

Procedure

A procedure is a document that is subordinate to a policy and is usually an internal or working document within the school district. Procedures are usually developed within a school district to address day-to-day operations as well as clarify policy statements. As a result, many procedures are multiple pages long and include very specific details about school district operations. Many school boards review procedures along with policies, but a board review is not always required. For example, a school district may have a policy that states the board's support of classroom technology and a student information system. The procedure or procedures related to the policy would cover many more details, such as password use, student data privacy, and electronic mail management. Like policies, some procedures are required by state or federal departments of education. An example would be a procedure that reflects state requirements and defines the types of scholastic data that are reported periodically to the state department of education.

Local School Policies and Procedures

Local control of schools enables each school to make additional policies and procedures to address the way teaching and learning is accomplished at the school. Discipline policies, dress codes, specific traffic flow procedures, and other "business" tasks are implemented at the school and sometimes codified. These local school procedures often include the use of technology, including cell phone use, computer lab scheduling, and media center technology availability.

The policies and procedures described above are all part of the scope of this text. For the purposes of this book, the term *policies* will be used to indicate policies along with associated procedures. There are some instances throughout the text that will treat policies and procedures separately, and in those cases care is given to differentiate between the two. Generally, school districts can develop their own definitions of policies and procedures, so consult with your local district to determine the appropriate vocabulary around these types of documents.

School technology policies establish the groundwork for implementing technology solutions in the classroom, at the school administration level, and at the school district level. It is important to identify and publicize technology policies and procedures to clarify the intended use of flexible technology devices, such as phones with cameras, MP3 players with recorders, cameras with Internet-connection capability, and phones with Internet browsers. While it may be easy to discuss the use of technology in the classroom, the expected learning impact for the students, and the benefits of standardized electronic data collection and reporting, the reality is that a computer or other technology device can accomplish so many different tasks, and without clear guidelines that are properly communicated, the potential for misuse of classroom technology is great. Each person using a district-owned computer, camera, personal digital assistant (PDA), or specialized device should understand the appropriate use of that device in the school environment and off campus.

For example, imagine a student who is using a district-owned camera for a yearbook assignment to take several candid school shots around the school gymnasium. With the digital camera provided by her teacher, the student chooses to take three pictures of a classmate in the locker room. Since the camera is so small, nobody notices her actions, and the student leaves the locker room to go to her language arts class. In class, the student asks to use the classroom computer during an independent writing assignment, and she uploads the pictures onto the social networking Web site facebook.com.

In this example, several school technology components were used to accomplish a task that is forbidden in most acceptable use policies (AUPs). Even though it sounds like an open-and-shut case where the student did something wrong, the legal perspective may not be so clear. Additionally, these kinds of technology uses are becoming more and more common, and the devices allow these types of inappropriate activities are also becoming more common. Therefore, developing, implementing, and communicating technology policies and procedures that have real impacts on students' and staff members' behavior and safety are becoming more important. Unfortunately, many school districts and schools have been slow to implement such policies and procedures. Paul McNamara (2006) writes in *Network World* that "despite daily headlines demonstrating the potential risks—as well as growing parental concern—most school districts still have no policy governing in-school or after-hours use of social networking sites such as MySpace."

Student Safety

Protecting students is, at best, a difficult job. Schools and districts that place student protection—whether physically, emotionally, or socially—at the top of their priority lists certainly have a challenge ahead of them. Schools and districts that protect students have often enlisted the wide range of school stakeholders, including parents, staff members, community members, and the students themselves.

The same groups of stakeholders need to be present in the development of technology policies, too. With the growth of the Internet and social networking sites, however, students are at increased risk in every area of their lives. In the article, "Teen's Vault to Internet Fame—Cautionary Tale," reported first in the *Washington Post* and again in *eSchool News,* an 18-year-old pole-vaulter was the victim of just such a risk. Allison Stokke had her picture taken by a track-and-field journalist, and her picture was copied from the journalist's report. Faster than you might think possible, Allison's picture was e-mailed, used as part of "lewd blog discussions, thousands of MySpace messages, a YouTube video, a fake Facebook profile, and an unofficial fan Web site" (Stansbury, 2007).

The lines between school responsibilities and parent responsibilities for student safety are also much more blurred than in the past as students receive more and more access to classroom computers along with personal resources. If a student takes a picture using their cell phone's built-in camera during an after-school event and then posts it without permission to the district's online forum and discussion board, it's not clear who violated the privacy rights of the person in the photograph. Furthermore, some school-related support organizations, often known as booster clubs, feel that they are outside the guidelines of the school AUPs and procedures. Pictures, notes with personal information, and defamatory comments are sometimes posted to these organizations' Web sites, so helping extracurricular organizations understand policies and procedures is extremely important.

Effective Instruction Through Technology

Designing technology policies and procedures that support the right activities relies on solid communication of what policies and procedures are already in place. If your school or district has not developed such policies, do not be worried—developing and redeveloping policies and procedures are similar processes. Most school or district administrators can articulate the expectations for appropriate uses of school or district technology, but without clear communication to staff members, parents, and students, misunderstanding will almost always occur. For example, students might believe that it is their right to access to their personal e-mail accounts on district computers. Teachers may feel that using their district-provided computer access to purchase personal items online is appropriate. The reality is somewhat different: Technology is provided in schools for the purposes of instruction or administrative tasks.

How can technology be used in schools then? As quasi-governmental organizations, public schools and school districts must adhere to the guidelines for use of public funds, such as those for technology. A public school board usually governs public schools and school districts, and a common practice—if not required by law—is to make financial disclosures to the public at various times throughout the school year. As a result, the public has input into the technology funding process to support instructional goals. Private schools may have more flexibility when spending funds, but their supporting parents and student communities often have different controls on the administrative spending patterns.

Policies and procedures also come into play when purchasing new technology for schools. For example, another aspect of policies and procedures in the support of instructional technology use are around the concept of purchasing and standardization of the school or district's technology environment. Instructional technology policies should also involve partnerships among vendors to meet administrative and instructional needs, because the vendors can provide insight on how to implement their technology within specific standards. Technology, usually an expensive addition to the school building, only has a limited shelf life and becomes obsolete within a few years. School technology policies can define the terms of vendor agreements, support structures, and purchasing or leasing cycles to meet the school or district's needs. Policy statements also govern items that are purchased using a bidding practice or public request for proposals. Putting specific items or requirements on bid lists to encourage vendors to address technology requirements also allows the district to standardize its overall purchasing strategy and the types of equipment that will require ongoing support.

As parents, teachers, community members, and students turn to school or district Web sites to find teaching and learning resources, policies and procedures can shape the content that is placed on school Web sites. Web development policies can clarify questions about a range of topics, including student work samples, photographs, and links to nonschool-owned Web sites. Without a clear policy or procedure in place, schools or districts can represent themselves poorly with their presence on the Web, betray student or staff confidentiality, and violate federal privacy laws or other information-privacy laws. School Web sites are also a point of exposure for providing the community with examples for complaining about the school board if content is managed carefully. As a result, Web policies often include a simple style guide, branding information, and even verbiage for specific schools' Web sites (Tiemann, 2007; Miller et al., 2005).

Amy Tiemann (2007) in the CNET news article "Is Your School's Web Site Revealing Too Much?" describes the importance of developing two-tiered Web sites that provide public information without restriction as well as a password-protected component for employees accessing information or students completing assignments. Each school and district must decide what is publicly available to parents and community members, and student confidentiality is essential. However, without some oversight and clear policy-driven guidelines, even the most harmless of photos and student information can become a source of enhanced photos and twisted news articles.

Finally, to maximize the opportunities for effective instruction through the use of technology, instructional technology policies and procedures should support nontraditional education, such as online programs for homebound or online students, educational kiosks, and self-service Web sites provided by the school or school district. As more and more schools use online and technological methods to reach students in locations other than the classroom, clear guidelines and parameters for using school or district resources should be identified. Teaching and learning resources on the school or district Web site can be valuable instructional supplements, but without clear definitions of Web use, regardless of the accessing computer or location, such tools can become discussion boards for bullying, complaining about school administrators and staff, and other noninstructional activities. In an article, "Schools Adapt to Digital Age" in the *Cincinnati.com* newspaper, the need for technology policy structure and understanding is described as an essential component of a successful school district (Kennedy, 2007). After all, the article notes, students are forced to move into a regulated technology environment as part of their work careers. Reporting from Kenton County, Kentucky, policies were changed to allow students and teachers bring their own laptops to school. Instructional technology, regardless of the owner, was deemed important enough to write specific policies to accommodate student needs (Kennedy, 2007).

Connecting to Learning Objectives

Regardless of the vision and mission of the school or district, school technology policies must adapt to the changing face of education and the uses of technology in the teaching and learning process. Policies and procedures should be flexible, not flat and autocratic. Otherwise, in an instructional setting, technology policies can become out of date as quickly as the computer equipment in the district's classrooms. Additionally, the policies and procedures surrounding school technology must account for innovation within the classroom. One of the best ways to prepare policies for innovative teaching and learning, for example, is to include a clause that defines approval committees or review processes for new technology. Routine approval of instructional technology by a local school or district-level review team would lend a level of credibility to new classroom resources as well as prevent redundancy in those technologies already purchased for student or teacher use. While a process like this may appear to slow down the adoption of new technology, a regular review cycle would help expedite the review activities.

Whether the district is more restrictive or more lenient in its approach to technology standardization of classroom equipment, school technology policies should address some fundamental questions and philosophical points:

- What is the school board or school district's position on classroom technology?

- What instructional purposes will be served through the use of technology?
- Is technology and instruction by technology considered essential to the learning process or a supplement to other classroom activities?
- How are students and staff members protected from inappropriate uses of school technology?
- What group within the school district is responsible for managing school technology?
- What are the consequences for inappropriate use of school technology?

Once these points are established, a school district has a solid beginning on or foundation for further technology policies and procedures. As noted before, a major challenge of developing any policies or procedures is that such documents do not always have a long shelf life and become outdated almost as soon as they are written. An annual review of all technology policies and procedures is recommended to keep technology policies and procedures up to date and make sure that they address current "hot" topics around technology in the schools or the district.

LEGAL POLICY REQUIREMENTS

In addition to crafting flexible policies, school districts and administrators need to be aware of the laws that pertain to the policies that they're creating. Most states require school districts to make their board-approved policies publicly available, and many school districts also publish their procedures. Unlike policies that cover financial activities, grounds maintenance, and human resource activities, technology policies have been coming under close public watch as classroom technology news articles, publicly available grants, and conference topics spotlight the power of technology in the classroom. Technology policies may require additional review by school communities and may also be reported to the state or federal education departments.

The Children's Internet Protection Act

As a federal law enacted in December 2000 (Public Law 106–554), the Children's Internet Protection Act (CIPA) is a law designed to encourage school districts to use filtering software, hardware, or other measures throughout school districts. The law also applies to public libraries; CIPA is a requirement for entities receiving federal funds that support Internet access. School districts must have a CIPA-based policy in place to receive telecommunications services discounts, commonly referred to as the E-rate program. There are three components to the legislation, and each of these three components may already be part of your district's policy and procedure documentation, but each of these items must be revisited each year that E-rate funds are requested. Whether schools or districts choose to apply for E-rate funds or not, the U.S. Congress has defined the guidelines around *appropriate use* for almost all public schools that are consistent with CIPA. The CIPA legislation states that schools and libraries must have

- A technology protection measure, which will filter out offensive or inappropriate materials from Internet users;
- An Internet safety policy, which includes provisions to restrict inappropriate use of Internet and technology resources; and
- A public hearing to adopt the technology protection measure and Internet safety policy.

More than that, though, the CIPA legislation was a groundbreaking move to provide local answers to a growing public problem. Regardless of the philosophical discussions about specific items to be filtered, schools and districts could no longer ignore the need to keep students away from inappropriate Web sites. In most locales, the local and state definitions of obscenity, pornography, and harmful content have been reviewed, updated, and revised to ensure that they comply with the public concept of appropriate.

As a result, schools are required to demonstrate their CIPA compliance on a regular, usually annual, basis to maintain their federal funding. Since the E-rate program is managed through the Federal Communications Commission (FCC), the FCC Web site is a good place to learn more about CIPA (see http://www.fcc.gov/cgb/consumerfacts/cipa.html).

Challenged by the American Library Association as unconstitutional, the CIPA legislation was upheld by the Supreme Court, that maintained the legislation is both constitutional and necessary (search for "United States et al. versus American Library Association, Inc. et al." for more information). Rebuffing their position that restricting information from Internet users is an infringement of free speech, the American Library Association was reminded that filtering could be turned off for legitimate research purposes.

As a result of this particular case, the CIPA regulations have become more prominently upheld in schools and school districts. Therefore, school districts must continue to develop policies and procedures to address the CIPA requirements.

The Family Educational Rights and Privacy Act

To protect the privacy of students and their families, the Family Educational Rights and Privacy Act (FERPA) was signed into law by President Ford in 1974. Like CIPA, the FERPA regulations must be met before federal funds are given to agencies, including school districts. Since its enactment, FERPA has been amended several times to maintain relevance to public interests.

FERPA is designed to prevent unauthorized sharing of student data only with parental consent or with the consent of students 18 or older. This protection extends to individual student information being published on the Internet or in other formats. Parents have the right to waive the confidentiality provided by FERPA, and many school districts have "release" documents to allow individual student information to be published, such as highlighting student achievers on Web pages or in newsletters (U.S. Department of Health and Human Services and U.S. Department of Education, 2008).

According to the U.S. Department of Education (2008), FERPA makes provisions for sharing information within certain guidelines. These guidelines allow educators to make informed decisions on the parents' behalf while in the care of the school. Personal student and related family information can be shared with the following:

- School officials with legitimate educational interest
- Other schools to which a student is transferring
- Specified officials for audit or evaluation purposes
- Appropriate parties in connection with financial aid to a student
- Organizations conducting certain studies for or on behalf of the school
- Accrediting organizations
- To comply with a judicial order or lawfully issued subpoena
- Appropriate officials in cases of health and safety emergencies
- State and local authorities within a juvenile justice system pursuant to specific state law

Source: http://www.ed.gov/policy/gen/guid/fpco/ferpa/index.html

Additionally, schools may release directory information, usually consisting of student names and addresses, to various organizations, including college and military recruiters. Each school district, however, may create its own policies and procedures to establish what information is distributed and the method parents can use to withdraw their students' information from the directory. Usually, this information is shipped electronically to various agencies that will incorporate student information into mailing databases, resulting in all of those college letters received by graduating high school seniors.

So how does FERPA impact school technology policies? FERPA is designed to protect personal information, and a great deal of student information is maintained electronically. Distributing individual student scores on a Web page, posting individual student pictures with full names, and publishing address information for students who walk home every day all violate FERPA regulations unless parents have given their approval for such activities. Unfortunately, all of these events have occurred, making personal student information public and placing students or their families at risk

(U.S. Department of Health and Human Services and U.S. Department of Education, 2008).

Another component of FERPA allows parents and students over the age of 18 the opportunity to review and request amendment of their personal records as needed. Although the parents may have a contention with the record, schools must have policies and procedures in place to address any discrepancies through a hearing process.

In an age where computers are so prevalent, printouts of student data can also become violations of the FERPA legislation if they are left on the printer or at home where other people can see them. Laptops that contain personal student information must be safeguarded through unique usernames and passwords from people who are not educating those students. In an Alabama court case, Appelberg versus Devilbiss, No. Civ. A00–0202–BH–C (S.D. Ala. Jan. 30, 2001) the daughter of a school secretary used inappropriate access to review the personal records of a classmate, illustrating the very reason that FERPA was enacted. Other cases include publication of student performance data on standardized tests, posting of student social security numbers, and several noteworthy cases where universities and school districts released significant portions of their data record to other organizations or to the Web.

There is one other concern in the topic area of FERPA. Social network sites, which are online communities of self-selected individuals, are places where students can provide a great deal of personal information without any oversight from parents. Instead of the school system giving away personally identifying information, many students post more about themselves than a school could ever provide. Pictures, comments, phone numbers, and even sexual preferences are all visible for members of the social networking system. Unless students are taught to protect themselves more effectively and restrict publicly posted personal information, the idea of keeping personal and family information private is just that—an idea.

As a result, school districts should develop policies and procedures to meet FERPA regulations, and then continually educate staff members, parents, and students on the importance of keeping student data safe and secure (Hart, 2008).

COMPARING TECHNOLOGY EXPECTATIONS AND CORRELATING POLICIES

When it comes to working with the varied members of a school community, there are expectations that each person or group brings to the school. When developing school technology policies and procedures, it is a good practice to remember these expectations and address them effectively in meetings and in documents produced for review.

Students' Expectations

Students expect school technology to be state-of-the-art and an open door to the rest of the world. As true as this may be within the home, the computers at most schools are several (or many) years old and filtered in accordance with CIPA requirements. High-speed Internet connections may also be available at the local coffee shop, but within the school, there may even be restrictions on what Web sites and online resources can be accessed. These limitations can come as something of a shock to students, especially to those who have a recently manufactured computer and a high-speed connection in their own home. Tom Regan (2007), writing for the *Christian Science Monitor*, identified a number of technology expectations brought to school in their heads, not their book bags.

Students also have the expectations to bring other electronic devices to school, including cell phones, digital cameras, and media devices, such as MP3 players or iPods. As electronic miniaturization continues, these devices are easier to transport to campus. School districts have instituted a wide variety of policies and procedures aimed at the control of these devices, ranging from a "technology items are confiscated" approach to the "just don't let the device interrupt the classroom" approach (Higgins, 2007). Some school districts have chosen not to address these devices through policies and procedures at all but allow the local schools to make decisions on what is permissible on school grounds.

One of the most difficult considerations to make when developing policies around small technology devices is whether or not these devices pose a threat to the learning environment within a school. Lawsuits and disciplinary hearings have occurred around the country as students have used camera phones to take pictures of standardized tests, posted locker-room photos on Web sites, and even provide covertly filmed teachers' lectures on students' personal Web sites as a criticism of the school district. In many cases, the goal is to keep students focused on academics and to cut down on cheating (Quattrini, 2007). Whether these activities violate FERPA or other laws depends on the specific cases, but the availability of such devices continues to make students, parents, teachers, and administrators nervous.

Teachers' Expectations

Most teachers want the technology in their classroom to be reliable and effective at supporting curricular goals. Being able to complete administrative tasks, develop lesson materials, and communicate effectively with others are usually the top technology expectations for teachers. The challenge with many teachers, though, is that they have very little exposure to the concepts of data security and view such concepts as an added work, especially where a computer is involved. Many districts have begun laptop distribution programs for teachers, giving them a tool to use when

away from the school campus, but have not trained the teachers suffi-
ciently to protect student data outside of the school environment.

Even though teachers are becoming more technologically proficient,
there is still a healthy attitude of distrust for computers, and no shortage of
teachers who are "afraid" to put their work on a computer. With the advent
of blogs, podcasts, and wikis, this gap of technology proficiency among
teachers has widened, and teachers who are only marginally comfortable
with technology may be unable to cope with the instructional changes necessary to accommodate new teaching styles in a student-safe manner.

Parents' Expectations

While parents often provide solid technology resources within the
home, there is a gap of understanding about what technology is being used
for teaching and learning around their children. The parents of younger
students are usually around when their children are at the computers but
less so as the students get older. As a result, parents are often unaware of
their children's activities using home and school technology. Students will
use home computers to post inappropriate comments about teachers and
others (Haigh, 2007), experience bullying or harassing situations and are
even being targeted by social networking sites as soon as they access the
Internet (*eSchool News*, 2007). Depending on their school network infrastructure, these activities can continue onto the school grounds.

Parental expectations of technology usually focus on the value of technology to prepare children to reach the next goals, whether those are standardized tests, school projects, or career opportunities. The school or
district must take responsibility to communicate the use of technology and
its impact on learning. Additionally, parents expect students to be in a safe
environment while at school, and this applies to the use of technology.
Schools and districts can manage parent expectations through open
houses, parent-teacher association meetings, and awards ceremonies.

USING POLICIES TO SHAPE INSTRUCTIONAL EXPECTATIONS FOR TECHNOLOGY

To look deeper into the use of technology in schools, the policies that shape
instruction are the most valuable of all, because they signal the purposes
of technology in classrooms and administrative offices. Each time new
instructional technology is purchased by the school district, the opportunity to use the technology for inappropriate purposes grows along with
the instructional possibilities. The incorporation of technology into the
curriculum requires a great deal of planning and preparation, and staff
members should be aware of the good and the not-so-good implications of
using the new technology.

Teacher Technology Literacy

Technology competence has been mandated for teachers by a number of state school boards and legislatures, which has required teachers to take classes or provide evidence of competency for technology use in the classroom. While this has encouraged many teachers to learn new skills and attain basic technology competency, such measures fall short of getting teachers to use technology on a regular basis in the classroom. There are two broad types of technology provided for teachers, equipment and access, and both require strong policies to help teachers understand the appropriate use of these components of instructional technology.

The first type of teacher-managed technology is equipment. With the advent of less expensive laptops, however, the scenario of the desktop computer for teaching and administrative tasks has changed. As noted before, many school districts are providing laptops for their teachers, encouraging teachers and administrators to use school technology for more and more tasks. Teachers are expected to bring the computers home in the evenings and on weekends, making many of the administrative tasks normally accomplished after the school day something that can be accomplished at the teachers' convenience. Other technology issued to teachers includes handheld PDAs, such as Palm Pilots, and digital devices for classroom instruction, such as polling technology. Projectors, electronic whiteboards, and even cell phones have become common teacher-managed equipment over the last few years.

Another type of technology provided to teachers can be summed up in a single word: access. Teacher Web pages, e-mail portals, and online teaching resources are all part of the instructional technology mix. Instructional applications, where teachers design online lessons for their students, require a clear understanding of the protection of student data and the careful use of sensitive information. Teachers are often issued usernames and passwords for online resources that have been purchased by the school or district, and should be treated as carefully as teachers' grade books.

Policies that support instruction from the teacher point of view often fall short of the realities of the instructional environment. Dozens of questions arise, and well-designed policies make successful resolutions easier. What happens if a piece of equipment is damaged through negligence? Who makes the final determination of negligence and then who pays for the damaged equipment? What if a student or thief steals a laptop from an unlocked, unattended classroom? What are the consequences of a student seeing—or even worse—changing other students' grades from an unattended teacher computer? Policies and procedures should detail the resolution of such events, along with many others.

Administrator Technology Literacy

The need for technology-aware administrators is continually growing. In her book *Critical Technology Issues for School Leaders,* Susan Brooks-Young

(2006) encourages administrators to focus on their vision for education, then find resources to support the achievement around that vision. "A realistic assessment of where your school is in technology use and creation of a useful professional development plan must be based on research on *how teachers learn to become more effective instructional technology users*" (Brooks-Young, 2006, p. 42). In addition to discussing specific tools, she continually focuses on the purpose of technology tools to educate and inform with a unified philosophy shared throughout the school community.

The unified philosophy for education rests ultimately with the administrator, who is the lead learning practitioner in the school. With the advent of multiple communication tools that are low cost and media rich, school administrators have the potential to reach more members of the school community than ever before. Ignoring the available technology will certainly not make it go away, but embracing it to accomplish educational goals can have rich rewards for the entire school. For instance, e-mails, video broadcasts, and Web sites created by the school can significantly improve the impression of the school community toward the school, building a pathway for increased school support.

School and district administrators are often connected to local school staff members through e-mail, making technology literacy a critical component for administrative success. Understanding the policies and procedures around technology can often protect administrators and schools from parents, students, or staff members with an inflammatory school issue. If education is the best defense against poor decisions, then this is doubly important for administrators as the public figure for the school or district. The opposing legal team, newspaper, or parent group could easily expose the school to wrongdoing if the administrator is not prudent with e-mails and other recorded communications and documents.

Consider a news article from *The Boston Globe*, "Officials Defend Tapping E-mails" where a principal and a teacher were allegedly sharing "jokes" between friends. A school district technician, investigating allegations of an inappropriate relationship between the two staff members, evaluated their e-mail communications. Lawyers became involved, and the legitimacy of the technician's right to read personal communications was questioned. However, since the policies and procedures were in place to support such activities, the technician had the right to review anyone's communications when needed (Beecher, 2007). Many school districts forget to educate school staff members about their rights and the risks of using school technology and that electronic communications are discoverable, especially where privacy is concerned.

Policies and procedures around technology can support the technology-aware administrator, just as a lack of understanding of school technology use can be perceived as an administrator shortcoming. Without a clear interpretation of technology policies, a school leader is left making decisions without enough background to make the *right* decision. In Thomas Hutton's article (2007) about the concerns arising around students' online activities, entitled "Blogging for Columbine," Hutton emphasizes the need for increased attention on student safety and appropriate use of online tools. Throughout the article, Hutton encourages increased awareness of teacher technology literacy and the importance of constructing a plan to use technology to meet instructional needs. Technology use awareness through nonscholastic media like MySpace, Twitter, Ning, Flickr, Tagged, and Facebook, Hutton points out, may have identified warning signals before a major catastrophe occurs.

Expectations of Students From K–12 to Postsecondary Learning

Often it is at the postsecondary level that the importance of technology policies and procedures becomes a critical issue. Adult students have earned a negative connotation when it comes to software piracy, illegal downloading of files, and misuse of technology, and offer suffer in the media as the source of piracy blame. On the other hand, colleges and universities, however, are getting smarter about using technology to their advantage or using it in a more positive way. "College Goes Wireless" by Melanie Brandert (2007) of the *Sioux Falls Argus Leader* identifies a number of ways that the South Dakota Board of Regents is aggressively providing wireless access throughout the state's college campuses. While this may appear to be a response to the changing needs of students, the increase in wireless technology on campus is a reflection of needs expressed by the K–12 community, too. In conjunction with the postsecondary wireless technology implementation, teachers, staff members, and administrators have all received training on using technology more effectively to complete their job tasks. Ideally in situations like these, training on the technology tools should also include a briefing on technology policies and procedures.

Using computer simulations of environments and characters that students design for themselves, called avatars, some teachers are using a Web-based tool, Second Life, as the location for holding classes (Sussman, 2007). Students can interact with one another and hold class discussions in this environment, although there is still a need for face-to-face instruction. Instructor Joe Sanchez, University of Texas-Austin, said that some students get frustrated that the system is not faster paced (Sussman, 2007). Other students may be intimidated by the technology, preferring more traditional learning methods. In the future, will students expect such experiences as part of their college curriculum, and will K–12 schools move to teach students these skills before they graduate high school?

Additionally, ethical behavior must be emphasized repeatedly to students to ensure that every student hears the message. As reported by Mitch Bainwol and Cary Sherman (2007) in *Inside Higher Ed*, college students alone accounted for more than 1.3 billion illegal music downloads in 2006. Unfortunately, reports such as these overshadow the positive use of technology in the educational process in secondary education environments.

Business Technology Expectations

The business community that surrounds each school has its own expectations of the school system graduates. In a recent poll of more than 7,000 Americans, one of the important keys to educational success for upcoming workers is the use of technology (Stansbury, 2007). Educational technology is viewed as an "equalizer" that can compensate for poor school conditions in the lives of students, providing connections to better learning opportunities outside the school environment. Some companies view the school-to-workforce connection as the most important long-term strategy in their businesses. Cisco, a major infrastructure technology provider, has even developed a 21st Century Schools Initiative to address their own corporate focus on building a stronger workplace. (For more information, visit www.cisco.com/web/strategy/education/index.html.)

In the workplace, though, there are policies and procedures to protect the companies' interests where current students will work in the future. There are significantly different consequences for not following the rules in the workplace, however. Businesses expect recent graduates to be able to use technology in a productive, ethical, and company-focused manner. Acceptable use of technology may not be part of a hiring package but is certainly expected of the staff members. Workers who spend a great deal of time using the Internet for inappropriate reasons or their work resources to accomplish personal goals may quickly find themselves without a job. Employers are also looking for staff members with a clear focus on ethical uses of technology outside of work as well, and more and more businesses are looking for personal Web sites of potential employees to see if the candidate is the right fit for the corporate culture (Davis, 2002).

Businesses also have their own policies and procedures around technology use as well, and experience in working within policies and procedures is a key expectation many corporations have for their employees. As a result, strong policies and procedures at the school level can lead to prospective employees who actively manage their technology use for the good of the company, not the good of the individual. Providing skills to balance personal and professional technology use are important, especially when students are engaged in a dual-enrollment environment, where students are on a high school campus part of the day and participating in college courses for the remainder of the day. Consistent application of school technology policies supports the student in any environment where learning is the goal.

SUMMARY

School technology policies are constructed to support the instructional and administrative goals of schools and school districts and should grow out of the broader mission and vision of the school. Without a clear understanding of the mission and vision of the educational institution, policies and procedures become empty rules without reference points and often confuse all levels of technology users, from the district administrators through the students and their parents.

Students' and staff members' use and understanding of technology in the classroom vary greatly, and policies and procedures need to be flexible enough to address these different expectations as well as provide solid guidelines for innovative classroom technology. Without a thorough comprehension for the way teachers and students use classroom and personal technology, policies will be unable to accommodate the needs of schools. Policies and procedures should support the unique uses of technology within a framework of keeping students and staff members safe while using technology. As evidenced by CIPA (laws protecting student Internet use) and FERPA (laws protecting the personal information of students and their families), the need to protect students while using school technology is a continual challenge.

However, by clearly linking the importance of providing safe technology resources to instructional goals, the entire community can support instructional technology policies and procedures. Acceptable use agreements are only the beginning of building community support for strong technology policies, because effective communication to parents, students, staff members, and business community makes the need for comprehensive policies and procedures even more significant.

REFERENCES

Associated Press News. (2007, July 18). Students filmed in locker room win case. *USA Today*. Retrieved July 23, 2007, from http://www.usatoday.com/news/nation/2007–07–18-locker-room-cams-N.htm

Bainwol, M., & Sherman, C. (2007). Explaining the crackdown on student downloading. *Inside Higher Ed*. Retrieved August 24, 2007, from http://insidehighered.com/views/2007/03/15/sherman

Beecher, M. (2007, August 16). Officials defend tapping e-mails. *The Boston Globe*. Retrieved August 16, 2007, from http://www.boston.com/news/education/k_12/articles/2007/08/16/officials_defend_tapping_e_mails/

Brandert, M. (2007, August 16). College goes wireless. *Sioux Falls Argus Leader*. Retrieved August 22, 2007, from http://www.argusleader.com

Brooks-Young, S. (2006). *Critical technology issues for school leaders*. Thousand Oaks, CA: Corwin.

Davis, D. C. (2002). Computer technologies used in business and skills required in the workplace (Master's thesis, Southern Illinois University, 2002). *Master's Abstracts International.*

Haigh, S. (2007, July 16). Burlington teen sues school officials over free speech issue. *The Boston Globe.* Retrieved July 23, 2007, from http://www.boston.com/news/local/connecticut/articles/2007/07/16/burlington_teen_sues_school_officials_over_free_speech_issue/

Hart, J. D. (2008). *Internet law: A field guide* (6th ed.). Arlington, VA: BNA Books.

Higgins, L. (2007, July 19). Michigan school district cracks down on cell phones, iPods. *USA Today.* Retrieved August 1, 2007, from http://www.usatoday.com/news/education/2007–07–19-schools-ipods-cellphones_N.htm

Hutton, T. (2007). Blogging for Columbine. *American School Board Journal, 194,* 14–17.

Kennedy, D. (2007, August 21). Schools adapt to digital age. *Cincinnati.com/ NKY.com.* Retrieved August 22, 2007, from http://news.enquirer.com/apps/pbcs.dll/article?AID=/20070821/NEWS0103/708210369/-1/all

McNamara, P. (2006, November 8). MySpace? What's MySpace? Most schools still lack policies for social networking sites, survey says. Message posted to NetworkWorld Buzzblog at http://www.networkworld.com/community/?q=node/9169

New social-networking sites target kids as young as six. (2007, August). *ESchool News,* 23.

Poll: One-third of teens are harassed online. (2007, August). *ESchool News,* 6.

Quattrini, R. (2007, August 8). Tech toys a turnoff at school. *The Arizona Republic.* Retrieved August 13, 2007, from http://www.azcentral.com/ arizonarepublic/local/articles/0808cellphones0808.html

Regan, T. (2007, August 29). The technology kids want, versus what they need. *The Christian Science Monitor.* Retrieved August 30, 2007, from http://www.csmonitor.com/2007/0829/p17s01-stct.html

Stansbury, M. (2007, August 1). Public wants more tech in classrooms. *ESchool News.* Retrieved August 13, 2007, from http://www.eschoolnews.org/news/pfshowStory.cfm?ArticleID=7268

Stansbury, M. (2007, July). Teen's vault to Internet fame a cautionary tale. *ESchool News,* 4.

Sussman, B. (2007, August 1). Teachers, college students lead a second life. *USA Today.* Retrieved August 13, 2007, from http://www.usatoday.com/news/education/2007–08–01-second-life_N.htm

Tiemann, A. (2007, August 28). Is your school's Web site revealing too much? Message posted to CNet News at http://news.com.com/8301–10784_3-9767326–7.html

U.S. Department of Health and Human Services and U.S Department of Education. (2008, November). Joint Guidance on the Application of the Family Educational Rights and Privacy Act (FERPA) and the Health Insurance Portability and Accountability Act of 1996 (HIPAA) to Student Health Records. Retrieved on November 11, 2009, from http://www.ed.gov/policy/gen/guid/fpco/doc/ferpa-hippa-guidance.pdf

2

It's Everyone's Responsibility

A Collaborative Approach to Technology Policy Development

Critical Chapter Questions

- How do policies and procedures complement the personnel in schools?
- What roles do students, parents, staff members, and administrators play in the development and implementation of policies?
- What role do technology team members play in the protection of students and staff?

Chapter Focus: *Explore the growing need for more community involvement in the development and implementation of school technology policies and procedures.*

❖

Charles, a middle school parent, was pleased to be asked to contribute to a special team focusing on the school district's technology policies and guidelines. As a parent, he enjoyed working with teachers and students on several technology nights at his school since he worked as a technology trainer for a job placement program. Charles supported his daughter's school by volunteering monthly, but he realized that the school was struggling with student cell phone use, inappropriate computer use, and a recently shutdown school Web page blog.

When the first meeting opened, Charles was pleasantly surprised that the school principal had already gathered documents from other districts and shared them with the group. "Think of these as ideas for creating our own starting point," the principal had said, "and think just as much about home technology as school technology. What we do here affects the lives of our students at home, so we must consider what students see off campus, too." Charles and the other team members, including several other parents, five teachers, and two assistant principals, were able to focus on the positive components of school technology, and the team was proud of their work. The team agreed that their policies and procedures were clear, effective, and enforceable, which means that they met their goal of creating policies and procedures that improved teaching and learning.

In the Drucker Foundation's Leader to Leader guide entitled *On Creativity, Innovation, and Renewal,* Costas Markides makes a singular point. "There is no reason why established organizations cannot embrace new strategies. As a leader, if you know that your strategic position will eventually come under attack, or that changes in the environment will threaten your standing, then your motivation is strong to be the one that develops the new strategic position" (Hesselbein & Johnston, 2002, p. 129). Clearly, the advent of technology in schools is an example of "changes in the environment" and schools, the "established organizations," must accept new motivations and new opportunities (Hesselbein & Johnston, 2002, p. 129).

One of the challenges that school leaders now face when working with their constituent communities is the need for electronic technology in the classroom, as well as a digitally designed public communication style with electronic newsletters, e-mail, and Web sites. When it comes to students using technology, emotions often run high due to the pressure parents put on their students to succeed, as well as unclear understanding of how technology is used in the classroom and for learning and achievement.

LEADING TECHNOLOGY POLICY DEVELOPMENT AND IMPLEMENTATION

Whether you are a teacher, a paraprofessional, a principal, a technology team member, a counselor, or a district official, your school community expects you to be comfortable with the use of technology in the classroom. If you are an involved parent, you know how far from the truth this assumption may be. Some teachers are outstanding users of technology, while some teachers are scared of the technology being installed in classrooms. Yet the pressure being placed on school officials and school boards to provide student technology is tremendous, and the funding is often lacking to accomplish this task. Additionally, the school or district policies to support technology use throughout the learning environment are neither comprehensive nor effective.

Regardless, as a school leader, it is important to set the stage for collaboration among all of the factions of the school community: parents, students, teachers, administrators, business leaders, community members, and support organizations, such as libraries, for school technology policy and procedure development (Creighton, 2003). In many cases, other groups or organizations can provide valuable input to support policy development. Businesses, for example, often have tackled difficult technology use activities already and may have technical writers or legal advisors who might be able to assist in the policy creation process.

Bringing all of the important factions together is not always easy, but the end results lead to more thorough and insightful policies and procedures. The same people who provided input to the process will also be stronger advocates of your school or district, and businesses will have more motivation to support the school district as well.

School District Leaders

At the district level, school policies around technology set the stage for growth and improvement of the district throughout students' time in the K–12 educational process. Leading the creation of district policies and procedures requires a close "ear to the ground" and the development of feedback processes to ensure that the appropriate resources are developed for all schools in the district, regardless of the level, such as elementary, middle, or high, or the specialty, as with charter schools, magnet schools, and special needs facilities (Brooks-Young, 2006).

Schools often face myriad responsibilities when encouraging students to use technology in the learning process, and setting policies and procedures are just one way to ensure that technology is being used properly in the teaching and learning process. Policies and procedures establish the school district's perspective and stance on such behavior as well as outline disciplinary procedures when school technology is used inappropriately. For example, emerging technology like iPods and other MP3 players can encourage student creativity and intellectual growth but can also be difficult to control. Even worse, students can obtain music and other media files illegally and share them with their friends, making the school liable for legal charges in the worst cases.

While many technology users perceive policies and procedures as a negative set of rules, the district-designed technology policies and procedures have the potential to identify positive and appropriate uses of technology, too. School technology policies should not be a long list of *unacceptable* uses; instead, well-designed policies focus on the ideal and planned uses of technology in the teaching and learning process, clarifying the intent of technology in the classroom and administrative offices. In

Alan November's (2001) book, *Empowering Students With Technology*, the author notes that "new technologies can leverage empowerment through access to new sources of information and relationships" (pp. xvii–xxvi). There may be no better place to describe the support of school technology use than in a policy. For example, the opening statement, "The school board and this school district recognizes the value of classroom and administrative technology, and supports the use of technology in the teaching and learning process," is a strong, declarative statement underscoring the importance of school technology (November, 2001, p. 1).

District policy makers are wise to include definitions of school technology and data components as well. By clearly defining the scope of technology systems provided by the school district, a policy becomes more inclusive and more effectively supported throughout the school district. Learning and administrative tools and data resources need to be delineated as the responsibility of the school district to manage and maintain, and reviewed regularly to ensure a comprehensive approach when developing new policies and procedures.

Definitions of resources and systems should include:

- Student information systems, and systems that store student information
- Personnel and employee information systems
- Instructional systems and educational software
- Online instructional resources, such as research databases
- Technology protection components, like virus scanning software and detection programs

Every district has its own "mix" of instructional and administrative tools, and well-planned policies include those personalized systems used in the district. For example, is your school district's media center check-out process secure, confidential, and backed up periodically? If so, then that system, which contains sensitive student information, should probably be on your school district's list. As a district administrator, you need to spend time emphasizing the importance of preparing policies that are as inclusive as possible (Conn, 2002).

Local School Leaders

Local school leaders have a double responsibility: Administrators must understand the scope of policies and procedures as well as identify and enforce guidelines set forth in policies and procedures. While this is not a job for the fainthearted, it is a key role of the local school leadership. Policies and procedures, especially those around school technology, may not take into consideration many of the uses that students and teachers perform. Local school leaders, whether administrator, technology coordinator, or network support staff members all have a singular focus to enable teaching and learning in the classroom, whether using technology or not.

When it comes to the development of new policies and procedures, local school leaders have a great deal to contribute. Whether or not a policy component is appropriate or effective really impacts the local school, so the "acid test" that a local school leader can provide by way of examples, cases, and day-to-day understanding of student and staff member behavior is crucial. If you have this responsibility at your school, then you also have the ability to draw on parental support as well for enforcement of the rules.

If you are a local school administrator, then your focus on instruction and staff support can serve as an invaluable tool for knowing how to identify a problem with technology use in the classroom. Furthermore, you have the tools to identify the right strategy for treatment by analyzing the initial problems:

- Are your teachers using the technology in their classroom effectively?
- Are they expected to use technology during instruction?
- Is a *lack of understanding* the real cause of problems when technology is being used in the classroom?
- Instead, are your staff members or students making poor choices when using technology?

Each of these questions has its own solution and can be solved administratively through existing structures, whether through staff development or disciplinary action.

If you are a technology team member in a school, then these are the challenges that present themselves on a daily basis. Especially if you are responsible for local school technology training, you must always look for methods that work with adult learners to teach them new ways to teach and administer their classroom. If you assist students in the use of technology, you must be one step ahead, providing clear directions on the best way to solve academic challenges and enhance the learning process. Whether the "customers" are staff members or students, you have many challenges to address, and providing input for technology policies and procedures can significantly reduce your ongoing issues around technology use in your school or district.

Technology team members and their knowledge about the day-to-day use of school technology in the teaching and learning environment are important members of the policy development team. Creating the framework of understanding for teachers to share with their students about appropriate technology use, as well as providing staff development to share best "safe technology" educational practices among teachers can make a tremendous difference in the school environment. A discussion of policies and procedures should continue to be part of the training for teachers receiving new technology equipment and resources in their classrooms. Helping students understand the importance of protecting their identity online should also be a small component of training provided to students.

Whether policies are made at the district level or local school level, the local school administrator and technology leaders have a great deal to contribute to the development process. Their in-depth knowledge of the best uses of technology for the classroom, whether instructional or administrative, can mean the creation of school technology policies and procedures that are relevant, appropriate, and enforceable.

POLICY DEVELOPMENT AND IMPLEMENTATION RESPONSIBILITIES

Ultimately, the power of creating school policies and procedures rests with the district superintendent and the school board, but there is nothing to prevent the development of local school technology policies and procedures. As quasi-legal documentation of the purpose of the school district and the use of technology to positively impact teaching and learning, policies and procedures require a great deal of preparation, both in terms of development and implementation. In addition to requiring a great deal of preparation, they also require the participation of many key players in the school community, such as school boards, administrators, staff members, and parents.

School Boards

School boards are designed to do several things extremely well. As elected officials in most districts, school board members can draw upon their constituents to get the public's response to ideas and thoughts. Board members are also positioned to implement or adjudicate in the case of hearings that support effective instruction in their school district. Regardless of the source of the policy or procedure, the school board's approval of policies and procedures means that they must "own" them to some degree.

Depending on the philosophy of the school district, school board members may have the ability to be extremely hands-on policy makers when policies are developed. In that situation, a strong connection to the National School Boards Association (NSBA; see www.nsba.org) can provide a great deal of guidance for school board members. Through conferences, training, and networking events, the NSBA provides specialized information for districts of any size, shape, or demographic. Every school board has an impact on the use of technology in the local district, and making policy decisions around school technology can either support or detract from the district's educational goals.

School boards also share a responsibility to implement technology policies and procedures, too, since boards must often decide what the correct course of action would be if a student or staff member uses technology inappropriately. For example, when a teacher uses technology to unethically publish standardized test scores, the school board will probably be notified of the infraction and determine the extent to which the teacher should be penalized. The same goes for whether or not cameras will be installed for recording disciplinary evidence on school buses or on school properties. It becomes the board's responsibility to look at the uses of technology, identify an appropriate policy to address the existing needs, and then look to the future for the best ways to enable teaching and student learning using technology.

Administrators

Administrators probably have the most significant role in the development of school technology policies, mainly because they set the tone and style of their schools. A technology-savvy administrator can, by example alone, encourage staff members and students in the correct use of technology within the school. Additionally, school administrators have the ability to provide feedback on specific policies and procedures that are unrealistic or ineffective as they listen to their staff members throughout their schools. The information gathered from teachers and other school personnel is part of a larger feedback loop that helps create continuous improvement in policies. An administrator's perspective is a more global one; instead of focusing on teaching and learning in one classroom, an administrator considers the entire school's use of technology.

In many districts, there are opportunities to review policies and procedures before finalization, and school administrators can positively influence the development of school technology policies and procedures at the district level. By reporting through their administrative hierarchy, principals, assistant principals, and administrative interns have the opportunity to reach the ears of the decision makers in the district. As principals evaluate staff members, they are able to see the impact of technology on student learning and take this type of feedback to the district as well (Creighton, 2003).

For example, if the school technology policies are too restrictive and the learning process is hampered by stringent restrictions, administrators will see this repeatedly in classrooms, labs, and other learning environments. School administrators will also be able to identify whether or not technology is being used for instruction or for nonlearning-focused activities, such as surfing Web sites, completing personal tasks, or time-wasting activities.

When considering implementation of school technology policies and procedures, an administrator speaks to the entire school community. Strong administrative messages about the use of school district technology, along with relevant examples from the school environment, provide valuable reassurance to parents and staff members regarding the public investment in educational technology. As the leader of instruction for the school, administrators are also challenged to understand the impact of classroom technology, which means that they must be conversant in the software and hardware found in the school. This is not always easy, but the positive benefits are great: By knowing more about the use of technology for teaching and learning, the administrator is encouraging new ways to teach and learn throughout the school community.

Staff Members

School staff members are often caught in an uncomfortable "zone" when it comes to developing and implementing technology policies. Without a clear understanding of the school or district's technology policies and procedures, staff members may think that their ignorance protects them and their students from poor choices on the part of the students. Therefore, publicizing and communicating the current technology use policies to the staff members becomes a very serious—and important—activity (Brooks-Young, 2006).

Some of the questions that school staff members need to understand clearly include:

- The definition of *acceptable use* for your school or district
- The role of a staff member in protecting students and other staff
- The extent to which technology and data should be protected
- The person or office to contact with further questions
- The legal ramifications of not following acceptable use guidelines

All of these guidelines will be discussed in subsequent chapters in greater detail.

Parents

Long considered the domain of schools and the school district, technology policies and procedures must become more of a parent-focused process. Parents often hear about the uses of technology—both appropriate and inappropriate—and can make strong recommendations to the principal and the district leaders to enable more worthwhile educational technology. Parental input on the development of school technology policies and procedures is critical, especially if the student is using home technology to complete assignments (Abdal-Haqq, 2002).

By learning about school technology policies from administrators, parents can more effectively support their students in the off-campus hours of the school year. Topics such as copyrighted materials, school-provided research tools, school-loaned equipment, and take-home learning applications can broaden student exposure to learning resources. On the other hand, if students are often complaining about the apparent lack of resources for after-hours learning activities, then the parents can suggest and support policies to make more resources available.

Another component of the parental role is monitoring student technology use at home. Without a clear understanding of the schools' policies and procedures, students may be using home computers to complete homework or projects unethically. Even something as simple as writing a school newspaper article then taking pictures of fellow students without a media release from the students' parents can violate school technology policies and procedures. Another example involves the use of technology to complete a slide show, inserting text or pictures that are copyrighted without requesting permission from the originators. Implementing school technology policies at home begins with clear communication from the school about technology use.

COMPARING THE POLICIES OF SCHOOL AND HOME TECHNOLOGY USE

In many schools and school districts, resources are available simultaneously on the network and at home. Instructional applications, administrative tools, parental information, e-mail services, Web blogging and podcasting, and distance learning tools are all becoming standard components of the modern classroom. Policies must address these tools, as well as broader, more global uses of technology that is not owned by the school district (U. S. Department of Education, 2007). What follows is a summary of key issues to consider when creating school and home technology use policies.

Access

Exactly what resources are available, and how is access determined? Many schools have adopted a roles-based set of access criteria, so that a teacher is able to access different resources than the parent, even though the connection tool is the same. In many districts, portals, or entryways for different tools, have been developed, allowing teachers to access e-mail and planning tools, administrators to use data research tools, and parents to review their students' performance data. Students may also have access to learning tools while away from school, especially those students enrolled in online learning programs (Tsai, 2007).

Resources

What resources are appropriate to publish online? Prior to publishing any tools online, schools and districts have to consider a myriad of different resources they could choose to distribute and the risks associated with distributing those resources. Student data, both individual and aggregated, receive protection under federal and state laws, and each tool should be thoroughly discussed prior to implementation. Student and staff information should always be kept in the highest confidence and that requires a thorough testing process by all of the potential users prior to distributing the tool.

Ethical Use

How is the information being protected by the end users once it is delivered to their computers or other technology? Once the correct resources and access strategies have been determined, the final component is education of the users. Whether it is a webcast, a student performance report, an absentee e-mail, or an online test, how will the users be informed of their responsibilities to protect sensitive data? Ethical use of technology implies ethical use of the data received with that technology, which means that an education plan must be part of the overall rollout. Some examples of ethics training that might be useful include public service announcements on-screen, mandatory training prior to username and password receipt, e-mail bulletins, online training, and even podcasts or video clips that must be completed upon receipt of usernames and passwords.

Support From School Technology Teams

As mentioned earlier, many schools have staff members dedicated to support of school and district technology. These staff members can become key players when it comes to policy and procedure development, communication, and enforcement by reiterating strong messages about technology use to students, staff members, and parents. Some of the ways in which technology team members can get involved in the support process follow.

Student Safety Education

Many schools provide an "online safety" class for their parents, especially in elementary schools. These programs vary, but they are useful in the education of students and parents about the correct use of district technology. Some schools even require parents to attend mandatory training with their children prior to the distribution of usernames and passwords. While this is not a good solution for all schools, student safety education provides valuable information for parents and helps support a message that the schools and districts are protecting their students from inappropriate technology use.

Community Resources Provided by Schools

Schools with community education programs and parent-education centers rely on technology team members to provide appropriate access. Prior to using any technology, learners in these environments should receive training and sign an acceptable use policy (AUP) tailored to their specific learning needs (Conn, 2002). While these programs may occur after-hours, learners will still be using district technology and need to receive the same training as other learners in the school. Technology team members, who are familiar with the programs being administered at their schools, can play a key role in this education.

Staff Education on Student Appropriate Use

Staff members are often at a loss on how to educate their students on appropriate use. Technology team members, including technology lead teachers or coordinators, school technicians, and school media specialists, all need to provide their staff members with training and documentation to help them understand how to protect students using technology. This may take the form of staff development, or it may be a topic included in each faculty meeting. It may also be part of shared resources, such as an online database, with materials to distribute to students.

POLICIES FOR THE LARGER LEARNING COMMUNITY OUTSIDE OF SCHOOL

Schools are a collection of community, district, and state resources for the education of our students, but they are also the center of many community events. One visit to the local football games at any high school will show how deep the community interest in education-sponsored events can go. Even throughout the school day, your community will be accessing school-related resources, from simply viewing a Web page to paying online for student meals to signing up for school newsletters and podcasts. For those reasons, the community must be made aware of the risks of children using computers as well as the resources available through the school district to protect their own children. There are a number of different "school-community" technology uses that your school or district can support through policy and student safety education:

Home Technology Use

In collaboration with schools, parents need support to protect their children after—or before—school hours. This support can take many forms, but parents are usually receptive to resources provided by their schools about technology use safety at home. Does your school or district provide electronic for all parents, students, or community members? If so, then targeted education about the use of these resources and safe computing can be promoted. Online homework resource Web sites, school educational media sites, and learning resources provided on the Web and through take-home technology, such as software, are all examples of school-promoted safe computing for educational purposes.

Off-Campus Student Technology Use

One of the most unique programs in some districts involves the partnering of local storefront businesses, such as groceries, and the local school district. As parents shop, their students can complete schoolwork using a computer and connection provided by either the school district or the business.

These types of machines can be considered a single-function kiosk designed for learning and should be configured to prevent access to applications and Web outside of learning applications. This protects the school district and the business, because students won't be exposed to inappropriate materials while in the business using a school-district-sponsored computer or connection.

Another example of this type of school-sponsored technology is school-designated "resource rooms" in public facilities, like community centers, where students can log into a set of machines to access the school network while in the center. This can be useful for accessing stored files, instructional applications, and homework resources. If your school district has purchased research engines, library patron tools, and enterprisewide instructional software, having a school resource room in a library may make good sense.

Public Library Technology Use

A similar situation occurs when there are partnerships between school districts and public libraries. Most libraries, however, have their own acceptable use policies and protective access constraints imposed on their computers and the access within the library. The goal is to combine the protection of the students with the protection of the general public, which often includes the same concepts. For example, both school districts and public libraries are required to follow the Children's Internet Protection Act (CIPA). The partnership between schools and public libraries is to provide instructional resources and applications for students when they visit the library. An annual review between school district media center and public library leadership of the acceptable use guidelines and policies may be all that is needed to ensure student safety. Additionally, the meeting may also spur additional opportunities for collaboration.

Community School Programs

Community schools, which are often held on public school campuses, are opportunities for public schools to become community learning centers. Community school courses in productivity applications, such as word processing, spreadsheet use, slide show development, will, necessarily, be conducted so that students have time using the technology to complete the course. In most cases, the regular school district constraints of technology access apply because the technology was purchased for teaching and learning by the school district. Class participants should also agree to an AUP for the classroom technology use.

Extracurricular Activity Needs: Academics, Sports, Community Literacy Programs

Occasionally other groups wish to use school district technology for causes parallel to teaching and learning for PK–12 students but separate in intent and leadership. Some examples include after-school activities that may need to use technology, such as writing clubs, math clubs, sports team registration, and community literacy programs. These are all associated to the students that attend the public school, but not necessarily core functions of the school district. Again, an AUP review should be part of the activity, and participants should agree to follow the district policies prior to using the technology. This may require additional effort on the part of the central office personnel, since many of the "staff" members in these programs are volunteers and not school district employees. If they are not staff members, they may be very difficult to reach during normal business hours.

INVOLVING MORE LEARNING COMMUNITY MEMBERS IN POLICY DEVELOPMENT

Introduced in the previous section, engaging the community in policy issues can bring community groups together to make positive decisions for students. One of the strengths in a school community is the fact that you have a group of parents, professionals, and volunteers all working together for a common cause: the education of students. This breadth of involvement means that involving more members in the policy development process will ensure stronger policies and more support in the schools when these policies are discussed and enforced. The following guidelines can help you formulate "task groups" that can be assigned to developing or modifying different segments of school technology policies.

School Staff Members

School staff members can provide feedback on the needs of students and other staff members when technology use is examined. Teachers are already operating with the students' best interests in mind, and policies should support their efforts in the classroom and not hinder them whenever possible. In the cases where specific Web sites or applications are denied due to inappropriate content or other reasons, staff members provide input on how to communicate such decisions.

School Technologists

The school technology team is in the perfect place to provide input on the staff development needs around technology policies and procedures. Often the communicators or distributors of the AUP documents, the school technologists have often answered many of the questions that need to be addressed in the policy and procedure. They may also be a source of instructional technology resources, such as "cyber bullying prevention" or "Web safety for parents and students 101" for the school communities.

Parents and Students

Parents and students involved in the development of policies and procedures can give candid information about technology use in the home and in the classroom. Input from parents and students can also be used to develop communication plans to distribute technology safety information in the district. Additionally, the involvement of parents and students indicates a willingness to listen and learn to improve technology use for all students and in support of parents' goals for their children.

Community Members

Some of the best information can be gleaned from community members, especially the business community. Many larger businesses have significantly more restrictive guidelines around technology use, while others have no restrictions at all on employee technology. Schools, however, have additional constraints from federal and local statutes designed to protect district students. Incorporating varying business and community perspectives into policies and procedures can provide a more realistic approach for defining *appropriate* access for students.

SUMMARY

In summary, the communitywide approach to developing policies and procedures has many strengths and advantages that positively impact teaching and learning and student success. Leading the development or improvement of school technology policies requires leadership, and sometimes that leadership's role is to bring the right groups to the discussion table, investing new policies with the wisdom of school boards, administrators, parents, and staff members. As a result, the school or district can move to increase access to students, educate parents, and develop educational partnerships through community education and staff education. After all, as instructional technology definition broadens into multiple combinations of hardware, software, and networked and online tools, learning can spread far beyond the school walls. A collaborative approach also implies a willingness on the part of the school or district to involve school staff members, school technologists, parents, students, and community members in the creation of useful, and effective, policies and procedures.

REFERENCES

Abdal-Haqq, I. (Ed.). (2002). *Connecting schools and communities through technology.* Alexandria, VA: National School Boards Association.

Brooks-Young, S. (2006). *Critical technology issues for school leaders.* Thousand Oaks, CA: Corwin.

Conn, K. (2002). *The Internet and the law: What educators need to know.* Alexandria, VA: ASCD.

Creighton, T. B. (2003). *The principal as technology leader.* Thousand Oaks, CA: Corwin.

Markides, C. (2002). The challenge of strategic innovation. In F. Hesselbein & R. Johnston (Eds.), *On creativity, innovation, and renewal: Leader to leader guide* (pp. 123–136). San Francisco, CA: Jossey-Bass.

November, A. C. (2001). *Empowering students with technology.* Arlington Heights, IL: Skylight.

Tsai, C. (2007). The relationship between Internet perceptions and preferences towards Internet-based learning environment. *British Journal of Educational Technology, 38*(1), 167–170.

U.S. Department of Education. (2007). *No child left behind: State strategies and practices for educational technology* (Vol. 1, pp. 16–17). Washington, DC: U.S. Department of Education, Office of Planning, Evaluation, and Policy Development.

3

Good Fences Make Good Users

Policies for Protecting Privacy

Critical Chapter Questions

- What information is restricted in the school environment?
- How are learning community members protected by legislation?

Chapter Focus: *Identify the legal perspectives surrounding school-related information privacy and its impact on technology use.*

As a graduating high school senior, Trina was surprised at how much junk mail arrived at her apartment each afternoon. Whether it was a stack of college letters and brochures, financial aid applications, or military service solicitations, Trina found humor in the irony that, now that she was leaving her home for college, she was getting more personally addressed mail than she received all the prior years at the same address. Trina and her parents also wondered how all of these organizations obtained her address, and her father even called the school and spoke with the principal. What Trina's father found was that information about students is identified in several ways: first, self-volunteered information on applications or entry forms;

second, data collected by the school that is legally disclosable called the student's directory information; and third, by data mining companies that sell contact lists to organizations such as colleges and financial aid services. Trina and her family realized that now that her information was published in so many ways it would not be easy, or even possible, to protect her information at this point.

━━━━━━━━━━━━━━━ ❖ ━━━━━━━━━━━━━

Trina and her family are unaware of the way student data is collected and used by the school and others outside of the school. If you are a parent, teacher, or administrator, it might be a wise idea to think through how your district or school handles student data and how policies can prevent data leaks or privacy infringements. The overall role of policies and procedures in the development of school and district culture is really to protect students and staff. In this chapter, we will examine issues and strategies related to privacy, confidentiality, and data protection.

STUDENT AND STAFF PRIVACY: THE POLICY PERSPECTIVE

Policies, for the most part, are quasi-legal documents that define and describe the business processes and the intent of businesses processes within the school district. As guidelines, policies shape essential activities and help staff and community members understand the school district's intents and goals throughout the teaching and learning process. As previously discussed, policies can also be used to limit activities that are not for the benefit of students or schools.

Probably the one place where policies have been evaluated most stringently is in the area of data privacy. Keeping student and staff information secure and protected has become one of the most important tasks that school districts can consider. Unfortunately, many districts may be confused or unclear about what data should be protected, why privacy is so important, and how to structure policies that are legally and ethically appropriate.

Legal Components of Information Privacy

The first perspective to be considered is the legal work surrounding information privacy. There are a number of laws, both federally and statewide, that apply to student privacy. Over the last few years, the issue of data privacy has become an important topic, and if there are also hundreds of laws protecting employees from the flagrant misuse or mismanagement of staff data, there are even more stringent measures where student data is concerned. Data privacy policies are not going away any time soon.

The first law that is quoted when school data privacy is compromised is the Family Educational Rights and Privacy Act (FERPA). As mentioned previously, FERPA was signed into law in 1974 and continues to be a major force in the educational communities discussing student privacy. FERPA's intent is to keep student data, along with the data collected on the students' families, protected from the public, while still making it accessible within the education community.

Another law that has an impact on students and their health records is the Health Insurance Portability and Accountability Act (HIPAA). This federal mandate requires all medical records be kept securely, and since schools capture medical information during enrollment or in specific care situations, HIPAA guidelines must also be followed. Especially in the cases of medically fragile children, medical conditions and treatment must be kept as private as possible.

When collecting information for free- and reduced-lunch programs, the Gramm-Leach-Bliley Act (1995) protects financial institution information that may be part of the qualification process for free lunch programs. While not as clearly connected to students, there are still implications to this act that require school districts to maintain strict confidentiality around students and their families.

Many states also have laws around data privacy, such as Ohio's House Bill 104 (2006) and the state of Washington's privacy laws RCW 42.17.255 (1995). These laws are often echoes of federal mandates, supporting the federal privacy acts and defining new components of state legislation, such as library patron data privacy, student data confidentiality, and parent rights around their student's privacy.

All of these sets of laws have one thing in common: all describe sets of records that are stored electronically, updated by schools and districts, and are all reported to the state and federal governments periodically. Even if it is just an assurance that the correct safeguards are in place, all of these measures—FERPA, HIPAA, the Gramm-Leach-Bliley Act—are part of the "audits" conducted by governmental agencies on a regular basis. Additionally, because schools are dealing with minor-related data, these measures must be shown as consistent and airtight, protecting students and their families as much as possible or practicable.

Student Information Privacy

Technology advances have made student information an easy target for information thieves. Unfortunately, many schools have not changed the culture so that students' data is protected at the school as well as in public. While FERPA covers students through its enactment, many teachers and administrators do not have a clear understanding of what student privacy really is or how to change the culture to be more sensitive to student privacy.

For example, consider the number of students who are involved in organized sports connected to a parent-sponsored booster or fund-raising organization. These organizations are incorporated separately from the school, carry out their own activities to raise funds, and support the students involved in that sport. Often, the teams will be featured on a booster club Web site, indicating students by both photograph and full name, and only rarely does a booster club ask the students and their parents to complete media releases. By linking to the booster club Web site from the school Web site, the school is tacitly endorsing the display of student images and work without the permission of parents or guardians. This topic is an ongoing school concern for many districts and will be addressed thoroughly later in the chapter and text.

Staff Information Privacy

There are two key questions around employee privacy. (1) What personal information is being distributed about me? (2)What information is being collected about my use of technology at work? These two questions are valid concerns of many employees, although many employees are unaware of the exposure that would be part of their lives if their privacy were compromised.

The first question, regarding personal information being broadly distributed, can result from a malicious act or an accidental act. Examining the sources of staff information is a good place to start considering breaches of confidential information. Typically, student information systems contain some teacher information as well. Another source of personnel data is the human resource applications used to distribute paychecks. Knowing what information is kept in these systems is a good start toward identifying those data elements that are sensitive, such as social security numbers, home addresses, and personnel records.

The second question regarding the use of technology of individuals in the work environment is often the subject of misunderstanding. Any resources that are developed with public funds or on public time are potentially subject to public review. Phone logs, e-mails, Internet browsing history, and saved files are all part of the public record. For the most part, these records are not examined unless there is a personnel problem or unless the documents are requested as part of open-records requests or legal discovery processes. However, most states' laws and most districts' policies make it clear that all records are searchable (Norum & Weagley, 2006–2007).

Defining the Use of Directory Information

In FERPA, there is a provision for a category of information entitled directory information. Unlike more sensitive information, directory information is the data provided to military recruiting, yearbook vendors, and school personnel. Typically, directory information includes students' names, addresses, and, in some cases, phone numbers. Schools or districts have the responsibility to make sure that parents can "opt out" of the directory information list, which would prevent directory information from being shared outside the school.

However, each school district is responsible for defining directory information, which means that directory information can include a number of different components, including parents' names, e-mail addresses, and even grade levels. While directory information may be distributed freely by the school district, there is a responsibility to the student and their families under FERPA to distribute this data in a way that does not violate other student protection measures.

MANAGING SENSITIVE INSTRUCTION-RELATED INFORMATION

Very few things will bring a parent into the school faster than an unexpected breach of student information. In one case, a parent volunteered in a school media center and helped in the circulation process. During a conversation shortly after her shift, the volunteer told another parent whose child had checked out books that day just what that student had borrowed from the media center. The other parent then drove to the school to complain to the media specialist and the school principal. While media center choices may not seem to be a massive disclosure of information, it was enough to upset a parent. Patron records in school media centers are protected documents in FERPA, and it could have easily been avoided by a short training of the media center volunteers.

Schools have a responsibility to keep student information private. Doctors must treat their patient information with the highest confidence; schools, school districts, and teachers must do the same with their student data. Even though there is a loophole through FERPA's directory information components, specific student data that can be used to identify students must not be made available publicly unless the students' parents have allowed this to happen.

In response to the amount of data being collected on students, a number of reporting tools that disaggregate student testing and performance data are available in the marketplace. Many school districts provide this data, along with the analysis tools, to the entire school district community. In addition to high-level reports, any user of the tool can "drill down" into the collection of data and review the information by different demographics and other indicators. This may violate FERPA if the data can be used to reasonably identify a single student. For example, if reports are disaggregated by ethnicity and there are only a few students in one ethnic group, then reports of this ethnic group may violate confidentiality of the students.

Parental Rights to Information

Parents have extensive rights to the data around their children. While most schools have clear guidelines around the release of data to nonparents, these local school practices should be enforced at all times.

Procedures are only defensible when they followed consistently, and releasing student information inappropriately is one of the most litigious areas in school law.

Parents have rights to examine almost all data around their children's school performance, up to and including teachers' notes, records of student behavior and performance, and all work products that the student has produced. Parents also have the right to release this information for public review, usually in cases where their children's work or image is being shown in a media venue, such as a newspaper, or a public demonstration, such as an art exhibition.

When students turn 18, however, they are considered legal adults and then they have access to their own records and can make choices about who has access to their data. While most school districts still recognize parental rights until the student leaves the school or district, students do have the right to seal their records from all others, including their parents. In the university environment, parents rarely have access to information about their child unless the adult child releases that information to the parent themselves.

Staff Rights to Information

Staff members have rights to student information on a need-to-know basis, which means that access is based on specific job roles. School or district administrators may be given access to all student data because it is required for the supervision of students and staff members, but the information available to teachers about specific students should be related to their levels of interactions with the students. Typically, teachers should have all access to records of students within their classroom at the time. That means that if a child is transferred from one classroom to another, the access to data for that child goes with the student to the new teacher.

There are always going to be exceptions to this rule, and these are governed by in loco parentis laws. For example, if a student has a medical emergency, all medical information may be released to paramedics when they come to pick up the student. Disciplinary records may be released to school resource officers or other staff members responsible for discipline, and special education records may also be released to regular education teachers working with those students. The wisest course of action is to focus on the need-to-know level of information for release to the students' caregivers in the school environment.

Another interesting consideration that is allowed under FERPA is the distinction between information learned from student records and information personally obtained by a school staff member. If a teacher overhears a student talking about illegal activities, then the teacher may report that information to authorities without violating FERPA (U.S. Department of Education, 2007). On the other hand, if the teacher shares information from the student record without the parent consent, then they may be violating FERPA regulations.

Student Rights to Information

As noted before, students' rights are precluded by their parents' rights until they are 18. Once a legal adult, students have ownership to their records, although they may not understand or use those ownership rights. Most K–12 schools continue to give the parents full access to records, and when the child leaves the school, the parents' rights end for accessing that information. Additionally, most colleges and universities only work with the students and do not allow parents access to any student data.

Students have the right to information collected about them when they turn 18. Prior to 18, students can usually work with school counselors or staff members to review their records. However, it is important to note that the school does not have to accommodate a student request to review his or her records; instead, that may be something that must be approved or requested by the parent. Some records, such as psychiatric records or other sensitive information, may be sealed to prevent review by the student, but that is usually done on a case-by-case basis.

GUIDELINES FOR PROTECTING STUDENT INFORMATION

So what can be done to protect student information from being exposed to people who should not see those students' records? Unfortunately, there is not a cookie-cutter approach because each school and district has their own methods for maintaining student information. As noted before, each state has its own records retention policies and procedures, but those vary widely by state. Methods for recordkeeping and safeguarding are also quite diverse, and a number of different companies focus on data storage and safety for school districts.

The most effective way to prevent student information breaches is to create a culture where student data is held as the most important records the school district keeps. While this may be the easiest way to maintain data confidentiality, it is also extremely time consuming and requires concerted effort from a number of different points in a school district. Some activities to change the culture include a series of communications for presentation at faculty meetings, surprise "quizzes" to ask teachers to respond to hypothetical situations around data privacy, and consistent messages about data privacy from leadership.

Changing culture requires a great deal of effort but is not impossible. The changes that are made to move a group of staff members to a new mindset will take several years to become fully entrenched in the culture, and reaching the parents and students will take even longer. The key to successfully changing culture is to provide resources for learning and passing on the message of record safekeeping in every possible context in the school environment. That might mean posters, roundtables, special morning announcements, bulletin boards, brochures, and many other quasi-marketing approaches that will help staff members internalize the messages presented (Marx, 2007).

Web-Based Student Information Protection

Training staff members to protect data is nothing compared to the effort that can be spent to teach students the importance of data safety. With generations of children who are totally acclimatized to the freedom of information access on the Internet, students must be taught the importance of protecting their personal information, even to their online "friends," "buddies," and "groups." While social networking tools are an excellent way to keep in touch with others, they are also an excellent tool for harassing others when relationships suffer a downfall.

To reach students, communication should focus on personal safety and maintaining anonymity whenever possible. Internet predators have become more sophisticated, using tools to triangulate data sets to find probable matches of personal data (Fried, 2001). Participating in chat rooms, sending others an address via e-mail, and using text messages to communicate all expose children—often at younger and younger ages—invites potential danger. This danger cannot be avoided because electronic communications are part of the mainstream youth culture. Instead, students should be taught that personal information exposure can lead to dangerous situations.

In contrast, there is a growing culture around being googleable by potential colleges, employers, and friends so that others can see what you have done in your life, both good and bad. This has become so common that students have even been dismissed from universities due to inappropriate information on Web sites. Blogs, wikis, social network profiles, and online reviews are all ways to connect with others in the world, and these children also feel that putting their information on Internet sites increases their potential for success in life.

Regardless of the students' approaches, an education program around protecting personal data is of growing importance in K–12 schools. A number of online alternatives to traditional classroom instruction on this topic are available (webwisekids.org, safekids.com, cybersmart.org, and others) to help build lessons around this important set of topics. Some are even developed into a game format that involves students in a simulation to protect other students from online predators. Many of these programs also have a parent component that can be used to protect students in the home environment.

Parent Communication Regarding Student Information Protection

As student data security becomes more of an issue in homes, parents will also need training about the protection of their children while using electronic communications. Strategies to educate parents can be extremely low-tech, such as brochures, PTA meeting discussions, and inserts in the parent handbook. However, some schools have had outstanding success by holding actual classes for parents around the topic of Internet safety. "Technology in curriculum" fairs, online and on-air public service announcements by the school district, and even online forums are some of the other strategies that school districts have used to communicate student data protection efforts.

Opportunities to discuss student data protection are also excellent opportunities to discuss the directory data released by the school district. With just a short explanation, many concerns around directory information can be eliminated. Parents, who have the right to deny the inclusion of their children's data in directory information, need to hear directly from school leaders about the use of data in schools.

THE EMERGING SOCIAL NETWORKING CHALLENGE

Social networks, such as MySpace, Hi5.com, bebo.com, and Facebook, are growing in popularity and use every day. The research firm ComScore (2008) provided statistics around Facebook in June 2008, noting that social networking is indeed a global phenomenon. Whether reviewing market share or the number of minutes users stayed online at a site, social networking sites provide a feeling of communication that is especially important to people who do not have much time to spend socializing (Red Herring Staff, 2008). Instead, social networking sites encourage the sharing of personal data, regardless of the age, gender, or shoe size of the user. In fact, it is more difficult to connect with others if you keep your profile with only minimal information. Another research firm, Hitwise, even looks at the geographic distribution of users to assess the growth in regions of the world (Dougherty, 2008).

In addition, social networking sites, which are driven by advertising, are developing extremely complex algorithms to connect users to one another. Unlike e-mail, where information about two (or more) computer users are disclosed to one another in a linear way, successful social networking sites have the capability to cross connect pieces of information that are seemingly unrelated and then connect people to one another based on that data (Bradley & Drakos, 2008). Students may enter information about where they were born, for example, and suddenly receive an invitation to connect with someone who was also born in the same city *and* went to the same elementary school *and* is the same age.

In the social networking context, there are numerous opportunities to connect with anyone else in the network, even if the emphasis is intended to be on "friends connecting with friends." Groups that center around specific interests, such as snowboarding, schools, technology, and religious movements, are prime "hunting grounds" for people who want to harm others. Although some of the more scandalous crimes are in the news, bullying and sharing of inappropriate files is a pervasive problem on social networking sites.

Blogs and wikis are examples of social networking tools used within a more instructionally focused environment, and they are making a great deal of headway as effective instructional tools—at least anecdotally. However, this does not prevent bullying if the students are able to contribute to open forums without review prior to posting on a public site. Blogs and wikis are a type of social networking that builds a stronger sense of structure around communication and messages. However, to be used in a classroom, the appropriate safeguards must be implemented.

Protecting Student Privacy

The challenge with protecting student privacy on social networking sites is that in order to have effective communication, some disclosure is necessary. Consider electronic "pen pals" where two classes of students are communicating with one another. Whether through a straightforward e-mail application, a blog, or a wiki, students have to be taught that there is some information that must never be shared with others without their parents' permission.

Another safeguard falls into the teachers' hands, and that is to simply review every posting prior to publishing for others to see. This is the most effective way to protect student privacy because it prevents students from making potentially harmful disclosures. Many teachers, however, do not realize that this responsibility is important for protecting the students using the communication tool. It can certainly create a significant e-mail administration burden on the teacher, but without the constant review, unexpected and inappropriate messages may be posted.

When posting items online, students should protect several pieces of information:

- Last names
- Ages
- Addresses
- Phone numbers
- Private e-mail addresses

Protecting this information provides a certain amount of safety, but a side effect of online communication forums is that people of all ages are much more liberal with their own information than they should be. Ongoing communication with students about using online tools appropriately and safely should be a priority in schools.

Assisting Staff Members to Make Appropriate Instructional Decisions

As noted before, many educators think that providing an online discussion forum will benefit every student in the classroom. After all, they can read their homework then contribute to the online forum in preparation for the discussion the following day. One benefit mentioned by many researchers is the "bringing out" of students who are reticent to speak or contribute in class (Yukselturk & Top, 2005–2006, pp. 341–367). While that may be true, simply having a forum does not guarantee that all students will use it properly, nor does it guarantee that only the specific students in the class will be using the forum.

There are a number of blogging tools and resources available online with a focus on safety and curriculum development, such as eChalk.com, Edublogs.org, ClassBlogMeister.com, and ClassChatter.com, all focus on using blogs in the classroom. With a little foresight and planning, even a generic blogging tool, such as Blogger.com, can support the moderation and access control needed to protect students.

If your school or district is looking for an electronic communication or forum tool, the following considerations should be taken into account:

- Anonymity of users: How are users' identities protected?
- Moderation: How will posts be reviewed by the teacher? Through e-mail or is the teacher required to visit the site to accept posts?
- Portfolio assessment: Is there a way to capture blog entries for review later?
- Public publishing: Does the tool support RSS feeds so students or parents can be notified of the topics of discussion?
- FERPA and Children's Internet Protection Act (CIPA): If advertising is visible on the site, is it student-safe? What information is collected about the user?

Educating Parents About Social Networking Risks

The role that parents play in their children's use of social networking sites is complicated at best. Some parents are incredibly protective, even going so far as to limit the sites that the student can access at home. Some parents are totally unaware of their children's activities on the Internet and social networking sites. Between those two extremes, there are parents who participate in their children's use of technology but expect their children to make appropriate choices online. Parents are rarely provided with systematic information about how to protect their children online, and schools are an excellent point for distributing this information to the community.

There are several ways to inform parents of the uses of technology for learning as well as the safeguards that can be put in place around home use of technology. For example, many schools host a technology open house night, where students demonstrate some of the learning accomplished using technology. Media festivals, curriculum nights, PTA meetings, and other parent gatherings at schools can become a venue for teaching parents the importance of helping students use technology appropriately.

If your school or district publishes a newsletter, include a short article about technology safety that can maintain awareness of a group presentation. A number of Web sites freely distribute information for parents to learn, and protect, their students online. Check out the Federal Trade Commission's Web site, FTC.gov, and search for "social network parent" for resources that might be useful. Ikeepsafe.org and Wiredsafety.org are two free sites focused exclusively on parent and child technology safety education. As an online extension of the school, these links can also be placed on your school or district Web sites.

SUMMARY

Protecting student and staff privacy is an elusive goal. Including concepts of data protection, information management, and legal responsibilities, policies should be designed with flexibility of methods but rigidity on purpose. Student and staff data must be protected, but there are always going to be exceptions to the rules, such as student directory information. Parents' rights to their student's data have become broader as more data tools are introduced, and more rigid, as laws around student privacy after age 18 become more of a norm. Culturally, teachers, parents, and administrators should be made aware of the risks of exposing student data even if that means that they leave a progress report on the school printer or a laptop screen open in a public place. Finally, students have to be aware as well, changing their behaviors to address confidentiality issues on social networks and what they volunteer in electronic formats. Regardless of the methods, schools have more guidance than ever before about data uses, but less about data protection. Policies and procedures are an effective way to shape a data-protective culture while leaving room for effective data use to improve student and staff achievement in the classroom.

REFERENCES

Bradley, A., & Drakos, N. (2008). *Seven key characteristics of a good purpose for social software* (Tech. No. G00159710). Stamford, CT: Gartner.

ComScore (2008, August 8). *Social networking explodes worldwide as sites increase their focus on cultural relevance* [Press release]. Retrieved November 18, 2008, from http://www.comscore.com/press/release.asp?press=2396

Dougherty, H. (2008, July 23). *Hitwise intelligence—Heather Dougherty—US: Geographic divide of social networks* (Rep.). Retrieved November 18, 2008, from http://weblogs.hitwise.com/heather-dougherty/2008/07/geographic_divide_of_social_ne_1.html

Fried, R. B. (2001). *Cyber scam artists: A new kind of .con* (Rep.). Retrieved November 18, 2008, from www.crimeandclues.com/cyber_scam.htm

Marx, G. T. (2007). Privacy and social stratification. *Knowledge, Technology & Policies, 20,* 91–95.

Red Herring Staff. (2008, July 23). *MySpace growth slips; Facebook rockets* (Issue brief). Retrieved November 18, 2008, from http://www.redherring.com/Home/24530

Norum, P. S., & Weagley, R. O. (2006–2007). College students, Internet use, and protection from online identity theft. *Journal of Educational Technology Systems, 35*(1), 45–59.

U. S. Department of Education. (2007). *Balancing student privacy and school safety: A guide to the Family Educational Rights and Privacy Act for elementary and secondary schools* [Brochure]. Washington, DC: Family Policy Compliance Office. Retrieved April 6, 2009, from www.ed.gov/policy/gen/guid/fpco/brochures/elsec.pdf

U. S. Department of Health and Human Services and U. S. Department of Education. (2008). *Joint guidance on the application of the Family Educational Rights and Privacy Act (FERPA) and the Health Insurance Portability and Accountability Act of 1996 (HIPAA) to student health records.* Washington, DC.

Yukselturk, E., & Top, E. (2005–2006). Reconsidering online course discussions: A case study. *Journal of Educational Technology Systems, 34*(3), 341–367.

4

Keeping Money in the Checking Account

Policies for Protecting Technology Investments

Critical Chapter Questions

- How can my school or district protect its investment in educational technology and infrastructure through the implementation of policies and procedures?

Chapter Focus: *With all of the funds being spent on K–12 technology, how can policies ensure the technology is being used appropriated?*

❖

Gerald shook his head sadly. As the manager of technology repairs, he has seen a shift from repairing overhead projectors to replacing component boards in the latest laptop models. Since issuing laptops to every teacher, however, Gerald's amazement over the creativity of destruction has continued to grow. Well past the "spill" repair when a teacher flooded her laptop with a glass of water, Gerald now sees more unusual computer afflictions from more creative teachers: a laptop used as a doorstop; a computer run over by a teacher's car; a melted laptop because the teacher, while preparing dinner, checked e-mail too close to the stove; a computer freezing up in a kindergarten classroom revealed that the teacher was day trading on her computer instead of teaching; a whole cup of coffee (cream, no sugar) into one computer; a laptop recovered from eBay as the teacher was trying to sell it; laptop screens cracked because the teacher stacked books on the machine; and the most recent case, a laptop infected with over 10,000 virus instances while the teacher used the computer during spring break. Unfortunately, his school district does not have a strong policy in place to encourage better care of the computers, and Gerald constantly talks with administrators to find out if the damage is due to negligence or occurs in the line of duty. Either way, the teacher does not have a laptop for several weeks, and Gerald wished there was a better way to manage the district's investment in technology.

THE REAL COST OF INNOVATION IN THE CLASSROOM

All schools are faced with the need to improve student achievement in every area, and schools are collecting mountains of data that must be reported to stakeholders throughout the county. As a result, schools are encouraged to innovate in the classroom, in the district, in the administration, and in instructional strategies. One of the key components touted as an *essential* resource for improvement is technology. Whether this means more administrative computers, handheld devices for the teachers and students, or door scanners to ensure students are in the right locations, technology is seen as a key tool for "fixing" education.

Classroom innovation, whether technology-oriented or not, is a costly task. Sometimes this cost is hidden, such as when a teacher tries (only somewhat successfully) to implement a lesson using a classroom response tool. The cost of inexpert use of new equipment, the frustration on the part of the teacher and the students, and the instructional time lost while trying to accommodate technology quirks are all hidden costs. You cannot assign a solid budget number to any of these costs, but the cost is there, nonetheless.

Alternately, some of the costs of technology implementation are all too real. The cost of equipment, and renewing that equipment on a regular basis, is one of the most significant budget challenges faced by schools and school districts. Even with insurance, the loss of technology due to theft or vandalism has a real price tag. The number of hours spent working with security personnel, the insurance company, and slower performance times for teachers and students who are affected can all be connected to a real cost. Of course, if the equipment is not insured, then theft or vandalism becomes an outright cost, due to the loss of equipment.

There are other costs associated with implementing technology in a school or district. Changing work patterns tends to create a loss of productivity at first, even if the change will eventually support student achievement more effectively. The tasks of "selling" the change to teachers and administrators may take long hours to address through one-on-one meetings. Professional development to show teachers how to use the new technology effectively has a high price tag. Preparation of facilities, such as extra classroom network drops, rewiring, and infrastructure revisions, are all expensive activities but required if teachers are going to support their students more effectively.

The reality is that innovation is an expensive undertaking. The classrooms of the 1950s were equipped very differently, but by today's standards, they would not prepare students for successful, productive careers. However, many schools are still operating in the modality of the 1950s classroom, and innovation for these schools has the potential to be unbelievably expensive. Schools must look for ways to make the correct investments, and then protect those investments so that students can receive the maximum benefit possible from that investment.

EDUCATING AND THE INVESTMENT COST OF TECHNOLOGY

Professional development is a hot topic in a number of fields, not just in education. Since we are educators, though, we look at professional development through a "classroom" lens most of the time. Unfortunately, that may not be the best model for teaching school audiences about technology use. Teachers are in an environment where the concept of education itself is changing, and they may not be prepared for the implications of those changes. A great example of this change is the blogging process around educational topics used to promote active discussion without instructor direction. Do teachers even know how to blog? Do they understand the protocols of communicating in this fashion? Do they even feel comfortable using a computer to learn something new? All of these questions are part of the challenge of new technology education models.

To protect your investment, the school community must be prepared. In his book, *The Principal as Technology Leader,* Theodore Creighton (2003) recommends a more unified approach to changing the school community through leadership: "Before we proceed with creating technology staff development programs, we must first agree about the importance of support and supervision during the implementation of new programs" (p. 48). Clearly, these changes forward with technology are not going to magically go away, but creating a strong model for implementing technology improvements in a school or district will have lasting, systemic value.

Reviewing various school district and state discussions about their technology investments seems to lead to a few guidelines that might be useful: First, for every dollar spent on classroom technology, invest an additional 50 cents on staff development activities; second, change the teacher evaluation model to hold teachers accountable for using technology with their students; and third, address the needs of teachers with "high flying" students, or those students who are not challenged by the current curricular models. With careful foresight, planning, and evaluation, each of these concepts can become reality in your school or district (Porter, 2005).

Protecting the investments around technology means that you begin by educating your staff, your students, and your parents and community members. Each group needs to be addressed in their own way to ensure a more effective culture-building process to share the protection of the school and district technology investments.

Staff Education

Staff members often perceive new initiatives outside of their comfort zones with mantras, such as "they are doing this to us" or "I only have a few years left to retire." To mitigate these feelings and change the culture in a more positive education, the school leadership, from the superintendent, principal, and assistant principal on down must be seen as using technology to solve problems (Creighton, 2003). This alone can encourage others to adopt technology resources for improving education and certainly leads by example. If the leadership knows how challenging the new technology activities can be, then they will help shape a process that fits the needs of their teachers more readily (Solomon & Schrum, 2007). The teachers then have a role model to follow, as opposed to forging their own path, which takes more energy.

Once teachers have incorporated new technologies into their classrooms, the need to protect these technologies becomes an important step in staff development. Even if the protection measure is simply locking the computer at night in a special case, taking a laptop home with the teacher, or signing an acceptable use policy (AUP), the importance of protecting the investment is a key component for effective long-term technology use. The point is, though, that the protection of technology assets, whether they are computers or data resources, should be part of the ongoing professional development for all staff members.

Student Education

Obviously, the students feel like they need more technology in the schools because they are part of a cultural revolution. In a report by the National Center on Education and the Economy (2006), recognition was given to the fact that schools need to "enable every member of the adult workforce to get the new literacy skills" (p. xxix). Students today are often underwhelmed by the technology provided on a daily basis in the schools because teachers have technology that is not used for instruction, only administration. Instructional applications may be useful, but without a computing device in each student's hands every class day, instructional applications may have a limited reach.

Unfortunately, many students do not value the protection of school technology and the importance of protecting it as their own. One look at the number of cell phones replaced annually—an estimated 150 million cell phones in the United States (Inform, n.d.)—implies that all users of technology have a "disposable" mindset when it comes to technology. Students must be reminded of the value of the technology and the implications of misusing or damaging the technology on a regular basis. This can be done annually through the signing of an AUP, the display of posters, the use of public service announcements, and other passive strategies in the school environment.

Parent and Community Education

The least has been written about the impact of community perception of school technology, but it is a growing topic of concern. For example, the One Laptop per Child (OLPC) program, a low-cost, connected laptop for the world's children's education, underscored the need for community involvement where technology investments are concerned (see laptop .org/en/). In addition to Title I funding requirements of having a community and parent literacy program in place, many school districts are reaching out to their communities like never before to change the face of education through technology. In *Oversold and Underused*, Larry Cuban (2003) notes that many societies may hold the following precepts to be true:

- Change makes a better society.
- Technology brings about change.
- Therefore, technology makes a better society.

Never before has the society been so ready to support effective use of technology in the classroom, but without the trust of the public, any technology-infusion initiative will fail. Instead, parents must be integrated into the classroom technology movement through the use of electronic media, communications, and performance indicators. Parents and community members must think of classroom technology as an extension of the community investment of technology, an attitude that is fostered by the incorporation of community members into the technology and policy planning teams.

DEVELOPING POLICIES TO ADDRESS THE CHANGING SCOPE OF EDUCATIONAL TECHNOLOGY INVESTMENTS

Hardware

When developing policies regarding the physical equipment related to technology, a keen eye must be turned toward the different forms of technology in the classroom. When developing policies, the emphasis should be on the use of technology for teaching and learning or the support of teaching and learning. If your policies lean toward "regulation of use" too heavily, they cannot be followed effectively in the classroom.

Laptop Computers

Laptops, while powerful devices, are also fragile and portable. Laptop policies should focus on the appropriate use of laptops, as well as making provisions for theft, misuse, and destruction. In many districts, teachers are expected to take the laptops home, so provisions must be made for home protection of computers as well. Here's a list of potential topics to include in your laptop policies:

- Purpose of laptops in the district and schools
- Protection of laptops
- Repair, replacement, and maintenance
- Laptop loss through theft, on-the-job activities, or gross negligence (including a definition of gross negligence)
- Administration of laptops

Desktop Computers

The standard desktop computer may still be the computer of choice in your district or school, and there are many considerations to make when creating policies for desktop computers. While theft may not be as much of a challenge with desktop computers, the typical desktop becomes a piece of "furniture" so teachers and students tend to treat desktop computers more causally. There are so many possible configurations with desktop computers that policies may need to include a set of minimum equipment standards for teacher, student, administrative, and computer lab machines. Standards help lower the costs associated with technology support, as well as provide a universal "look and feel" to keep students and staff members comfortable around technology. Below are some potential topics around desktop computer policies:

- Equipment standards
- File transfers among machines
- Networking guidelines
- Access control (e.g., who is allowed to use specific machines)
- Repair, replacement, and maintenance processes

Handheld Devices

With the evolution of the handheld device, such as BlackBerry, Pocket PC, iPod, and Palm tools, an entire education-focused market has emerged around the use of these devices in schools and districts. The Harvard

Graduate School of Education and Harvard Extension School even has a project focused on the use of these tools, entitled the Handheld Devices for Ubiquitous Learning (HDUL) project. Funded by Harvard's provost, this project sought to determine how wireless handheld devices—which include, but are not limited to, cell phones, personal digital assistants, and mobile gaming devices—could enhance learning and teaching (see http://gseacademic.harvard.edu/~hdul/). While primarily focused in the university setting, the implications for K–12 use of these devices are more widespread. Platforms for handheld devices are diverse and dynamic, making it very difficult for a school or district to standardize on a specific tool or operating system. In "Unlocking the learning value of wireless mobile devices," Jeremy Roschelle (2003) emphasizes the importance of planning carefully for these tools in the classroom, by "finding the combinations in which the unique, powerful, and reliable capabilities of [wireless tools] enable and motivate the unique, powerful, and reliable properties of social interaction . . ." (pp. 260–272).

Below are some potential topics for policies that address handheld tools:

- Proper care and use guidelines
- Equipment standards and proposed educational uses
- File transfers among devices
- Access control
- Limits of use and acceptable use, including cameras, voice recorders, infrared controllers, etc.
- Repair, replacement, and maintenance processes

Other Devices

In schools, this category of hardware is the most nebulous. Projectors, printers, SmartBoards, multifunction devices, adaptive technology, audio-visual devices, cameras, and even voice amplification devices are all becoming part of the teacher's classroom toolset. Policies are difficult to write in this area because instructional technology in this category is an ever-changing mix of tools, techniques, and vendors. However, when developing policies for these items, consider including the following:

- Ownership and anticipated use of the tools
- Protection, care and maintenance of the equipment
- Sharing of the device(s) among teachers or schools
- Repair of the technology

Software

In the world of instructional technology, software has become an incredible asset that differentiates instruction, supplements classroom learning, and provides for the administration of hundreds of thousands of classrooms. The software assets of schools need protection, too, in terms of appropriate use, license management, and version maintenance. The flexibility of classroom technology, combined with robust information systems, make software and the output of software more sensitive than ever. The following categories of software—instructional, administrative, and infrastructure—all require a different approach to policies and procedures.

Instructional Applications

Software for the teaching and learning of students (and sometimes parents and community members) can be powerful assets for the classroom. On the other hand, such applications can hold data without proper security in place, creating a risk for all students using the application. Instructional applications typically go through two reviews prior to implementation in the classroom: a hardware compatibility review and a curriculum materials review. However, every school teacher who has attended a teaching conference in the last 10 years has been offered free classroom software. Those *free* applications that teachers install on their classroom computer without review may be the most dangerous of all and may cost the school district thousands or millions of dollars. How? Well, some software creates security risks for the network, some report student performance data back to a "mother ship" program that aggregates the data for the company's purposes, and some software also displays adware and opens the network up to viruses. Therefore, when crafting policies for instructional applications, the following concepts should be considered:

- Software licensing (Is there one? What are the terms?)
- Intended use of the application
- Data collected
- Data security
- Software review process
- Management and maintenance of the software
- Removal of unapproved software
- Support of software

Administrative Applications

Administrative applications include productivity tools, student information systems, e-mail, media center management applications, and data reporting tools. The first concern with any administrative applications is the security of the data that they hold. Of course, such applications are only secure if the software users work to keep the data safe as well. While the culture around policies and procedures will be discussed more fully in Chapter 7, school technology policies should still focus on the sanctity of student data at all times. In fact, this is required by Family Educational Rights and Privacy Act (FERPA), but school district staff should be regularly reminded that it is their responsibility to protect student information, regardless of how it is being displayed, e.g., printouts, screen shots, e-mails, individualized education plan (IEP) applications databases, teacher Web sites, etc. Consider the following concepts for your administrative application policies:

- Data security emphasis
- Available applications and intent of use
- Data availability (need to know, right to know, etc.)
- Support structure for applications
- Backup and administration

Portal Applications

More and more schools and districts are turning to a portal approach, which allows a single sign on for a number of personalized district resources. For example, using a portal, a teacher might be able to access her e-mail, request resources from the school media center, review past pay stubs, and review assessment information for the students in her class. A student might use a portal to look at grades, submit schoolwork, and complete homework assignments from his teachers. A parent might use a portal to review her child's grades, communicate with her child's teachers, review attendance, and prepay on school lunch accounts. Each "version" of the portal, regardless of the user, needs to be accompanied by a signed (either physically or digitally) AUP. With such a policy, users agree to access the portal along the lines of the school district's existing policies and procedures. A strong portal protection policy includes the following:

- District intent for providing the portal
- Management of usernames and passwords
- Information available through the portal
- Access guidelines for the portal

Infrastructure

The term *infrastructure* includes the overarching resources that must be available to use technology for teaching and learning or the administration of teaching and learning; protecting the infrastructure often means protecting the circulatory system of the school. Without e-mail, data applications, instructional applications, and administrative software, schools are plunged back into the teaching process of the 1800s. Therefore, keeping the school and district technology infrastructure "healthy" is a top priority.

Network Connections

How computers are connected to the network needs to be clearly defined and, in some cases, should be defined by types of devices and roles of the users. For example, the connection of a "smart whiteboard" to the network may be different than the connection of a computer, which is different than the connection of a wireless shared printer. A principal may need to have different access to the network than the school technology administrator (in fact, I hope that they do!), and the media specialist may need another type of network access. There is also a software component to the network connection kept on the machines themselves. Are some users able to log into any machine in the school or just to certain computers assigned to them specifically? Each of these questions and concepts should be addressed when developing policies and procedures around network access:

- Intent of network connections
- Breadth of devices to be connected
- Standards for classroom access
- Roles and purposes of technology users
- Precautions taken for unauthorized network connections

Wireless Infrastructure

If your school or district uses a wireless network or overlay, then additional attention must be given to the use of the wireless network. Who has access rights? How do they connect to the network wirelessly? What services are available via the wireless network? Wireless networks may also facilitate the use of student response devices, projection devices, printers, and other peripheral technology. While these ideas may all be answered through wireless technology development process, review the following concepts as well:

- Access to the wireless network (for both devices and users)
- Intent of wireless connections
- How wireless connections differ from wired network connections
- Security of the wireless network
- Support of wireless connections
- Applications available through the wireless network

Servers

Servers, as part of the network, are a shared resource containing district- or school-specified data. Unlike a personal computer or device, servers usually have a number of different developers who have access to the server and the data. For example, a school might have a local server for its student information system, and each night, the data is transmitted to the school district server. In reality, both the local school and the district user have some responsibility for the data and maintenance on both servers. Servers are also used for multiple purposes, providing data and tools for several different applications, which make the maintenance process more complicated. Consider the following ideas when creating server policies:

- Server infrastructure overview
- Server security and access

- Maintenance and upgrades
- Overall server administration (Who assigns access to servers on the network?)

Portals

As discussed before, portals are an aggregation of a variety of different applications, each of which may have a different business owner in the school district. Like servers, portals provide a mix of data and tools, and so the implementation of portals also requires a collaborative approach for development. To make matters more confusing, there may also be separate support groups for each tool included in the portal. In addition to the previous portal and server guidelines mentioned above, review the following when developing policies:

- Portal administration
- Ownership of portal applications
- Support of portal applications

Virtual Resources, Such as Online Applications

This is probably one of the most difficult topics to address today in school technology because more and more districts are purchasing services instead of owning the equipment and resources themselves. This can be a source of great relief for the district, but it can also be a significant headache if not managed properly. For many of these applications, sensitive student data is going outside of the district and now resides on a server in another part of the world. Without appropriate attention, student information may be exposed or used inappropriately by companies contracted to provide services.

Purchased Services, Including Research Tools

The area of purchased services has emerged as a strong offering from many business sectors. Everything from Internet filters to media research tools to e-mail management to finance applications is available through the Web for school districts. Where these services interact with school technology policies and procedures is usually around the security of data. Is data being kept as securely as it is in the school district? Are FERPA and Children's Internet Protection Act (CIPA) guidelines being implemented in the use of the offered services? For whom are these applications provided: school personnel, district personnel, all staff, student, or community member? Policies and procedures can help define safe guidelines around the types of vendors you should invite to work with your school system:

- Goal of purchasing applications (favorable costs, unique services, better use of resources, etc.)
- Security required by the school district

- Management of FERPA, CIPA, and, in some cases Health Insurance Portability and Accountability Act (HIPAA) guidelines
- Access to purchased services

Online Learning Applications

Relative newcomers to the education scene, online learning applications have been used in business for many years. However, by entering the school market, online learning application providers have changed their products to offer student-information-like tools that integrate with existing school applications. Much like purchased services, security must be appropriate for the handling of school data, and many of these applications must be able to integrate with school data for class rosters, attendance, and grade reporting. Online learning applications may need to be reviewed extremely carefully in the area of student-to-student interaction to prevent inappropriate communications among students. Bullying and harassment can occur in an online learning application if proper care is not taken to prevent such student behaviors. Reviewing the concepts below when evaluating online learning tool policies:

- Intent of online learning at the school or district
- Appropriate use of the tool by students and staff members
- Data collected and reported by the online learning system
- Security of data
- Integration with existing student information systems and learning management systems

SUMMARY

When school districts make an investment in technology, their goal is to provide a sustainable source of educational innovation and teaching and learning tools. Policies can help protect this investment, but staff, students, and even parent and community members must be educated about the rationale and the value of the technology placed in the schools. Creating or revising policies and procedures to change with the technology can be something of a challenge, especially considering how rapidly hardware, software, infrastructure, and hybrid virtual resources can all change. Policies should be reviewed annually to ensure that they are properly addressing a range of challenges, including vandalized computers, negligence of portable technology, stolen or pirated software, unauthorized networking devices, and the uses of online research tools and portals. Ideally, the policies should be living documents for the technology teams, administrators, and other technology support personnel because they will use the policies to manage the district's resources more effectively.

REFERENCES

Creighton, T. (2003). *The principal as technology leader.* Thousand Oaks, CA: Corwin.

Cuban, L. (2003). *Oversold and underused computers in the classroom.* New York: Harvard University Press.

Inform. Cell phones FAQ. (n.d.). *The Secret Life Series.* Retrieved April 6, 2009, from http://www.secret-life.org/cellphones/cell_FAQ.php

National Center on Education and the Economy (2006). *Tough choices or tough times: The report of the New Commission on the Skills of the American Workforce.* San Francisco, CA: Jossey-Bass.

Porter, B. E. (2005). Time and implementing changes. *British Journal of Educational Technology, 36*(6), 1063–1065.

Roschelle, J. (2003). Unlocking the learning value of wireless mobile devices. *Journal of Computer Assisted Learning, 19*(3), 260–272.

Schrum, L., & Solomon, G. (2007). *Web 2.0: New tools, new schools.* Washington, DC: International Society for Technology in Education.

5

Knowing the Secret Handshake

Technology Access Policies

Critical Chapter Questions

- How should an acceptable use policy (AUP) be structured?
- What is the role of the password in my organization? Who receives access to specific systems?

Chapter Focus: *Explore methods for designing and implementing a student, staff, and community access strategy.*

Margaret was excited to be starting a new school year. As an elementary teacher, she reflected, there is always something energizing about new students, new teaching opportunities, and even new colleagues. Over the summer another exciting change occurred at her school: Every classroom had brand-new computers and she would be receiving a laptop. During preplanning, her school technology team led a discussion on new learning tools on the classroom computers. One topic that was also discussed was something called an acceptable use policy (AUP). This

document was something to be signed by every teacher, every student, and every staff member. Margaret read through it carefully, wondering if there was a "school Internet police squad" watching her every move on the computer but chose not to ask that question in the larger group. After the meeting some of her colleagues, however, were not happy with the AUP, stating that they felt the document undermined morale because the teachers were not trusted to use computers appropriately. While Margaret felt that it was a good idea to sign the document, she could also see the point her colleagues were making. However, she knew that her signature was simply an assurance that she had been trained and the rules had been discussed, not a restriction on what she could do on a computer. After all, if signing an AUP was her biggest worry as the school year started, it was going to be a great year!

Comparing school and district activities to what really needs to happen in the classroom in the process for teaching and learning can be a difficult process but not impossible. This chapter provides some guidelines for evaluating the current "state of affairs" in your policies around technology access. The focus of the following comments is really on instruction and the administration of teaching in learning in schools.

EVALUATING SCHOOL TECHNOLOGY FUNCTIONS AND RELATED POLICIES

Schools typically follow a set of guidelines around technology whether those guidelines are formalized into a policy or kept in the tacit understanding of the staff members. To protect the school and district, however, it is important to codify the major expectations around technology use for staff members, students, parents, and community members.

• *E-mail applications.* In *IT Governance Policies and Procedures*, Michael Wallace and Larry Webber (2008) note that, for e-mail, "irresponsible use reduces their availability for critical business operations, compromises corporate security and network integrity, and leaves the company open to potentially damaging litigation" (p. 601). If that is true for business, it is even more impactful for schools and districts, which must consider Family Educational Rights and Privacy Act (FERPA) and Children's Internet Protection Act (CIPA) guidelines as well. Wallace and Webber's (2008) strategy focuses on the clear definition of the value of e-mail to the organization, as well as defining clear standards around e-mail, such as e-mail account rights, e-mail etiquette, copyright components (i.e., who owns the e-mail?), the impact of e-mail on the overall network, and the ability to delegate readership and editing rights to others. Another component to include in policies regarding e-mail is a clear description of penalties for violating the agreement. Does the policy place the responsibility of communications from your e-mail system on the individual user or does the school district assume ownership of the communication from a staff member? Another consideration is to define spam e-mails clearly and how to handle such messages as a staff member. Finally, clearly delineate the privacy rights of the individual. In many states, e-mails are fully disclosable upon a public records request or investigation.

- *Internet access—both intranet and Internet.* In many schools and districts, Internet access has been expected as a right, not a privilege or a work resource. Unfortunately, there are education professionals who lose their jobs annually because they demonstrated a pattern of inappropriate Internet use. While many teachers, schools, and districts are using technology to generate more highly qualified teachers than ever before, the expectation that schools both use and generate high-quality information in the teaching and learning process (Keller, 2006). Therefore, Internet-related policies should be developed with two foci: access to Internet-based information and the creation of Internet-delivered information.

When viewing Web sites through school district resources, is your school district going to differentiate access between staff members, teachers, and students? What resources will be available through the intranet and which resources have the district purchased for administrative, teacher, or student use? How will Web use be monitored and is this data archived or deleted periodically? In addition to answering these questions, policies may want to connect clearly to the state or governing agency's professional ethics standards that address using technology appropriately.

In terms of developing Web content, many staff members will need some instruction on what is appropriate and permissible to place on a Web page. Even if the Web page is deemed "private," there are still security risks, and Internet policies should include guidelines on safely using discussion tools "defensive poster" on the Internet (adopting the paradigm of safety from defensive driving) with the use of media release forms. Student work that is posted on a district, school, or teacher Web page should always be accompanied by a signed media release form so the district has an assurance that the parent is comfortable with their student's image or work publicly displayed. Like e-mail, copyright, readability, and usability should be part of the policy.

- *Instructional applications.* Defining access to teaching and learning applications can be very complex, considering the breadth of instructional software. Policies should focus on distribution of access, administration of access and data, and intent of the software within the district or school. Consider defining instructional software as core curriculum or supplemental learning materials, so that teachers understand the flexibility they have in planning lessons using technology. If the instructional application is a purchased service, define the collection, use, and ownership of data gathered by the software as well, and identify the administrative groups that have access to the data.

• *Administrative systems.* Human resource applications, finance tools, media program patron systems, and even school check-in and check-out systems all require specific policies for accessing. In these cases, the policies held by the school and district may be legally defined due to the responsibilities of different staff members in the school. Support employees, such as school clerical personnel, may need to have multiple accesses to manage the affairs assigned to administrators. The school secretary may need to hold the same access to administrative software as the principal, depending on job responsibilities, so a careful evaluation of workflow processes should be conducted prior to defining or redefining access.

• *Student information application.* The student information system is one of the most critical applications in the school district because the data collected in these systems is used for state and federal reporting, curriculum planning, and school organization. With many school information applications, there are multiple views or access levels into the system. For example, a teacher may have one view for taking attendance, viewing student data, and entering grades, while the principal may have another view for evaluating test scores by grade level and classroom. Still another access level may be the local school data administrator who has full editing rights to enter, remove, and edit student information. Even parents may be able to access some of the data to verify student addresses, names, and related data.

• *School system information.* In its efforts to communicate to the community, many districts place extensive information about the system online, including school addresses, opening and closing times, calendars, bus schedules, school board minutes, and even recognition articles for students and teachers. School system information should be carefully monitored and held to a high standard of usability. System Web sites may also contain links to portal applications, instructional software, blogs, online campus Web sites, and state education Web sites. Each of the links must be thoroughly tested to ensure appropriate material is being presented by the district. Policies for the district Web site should clearly delineate the responsibilities for posting information, managing Web site design, and assuring the content on the Web site.

On a side note, school district blogs may not be a wise idea, since information posted on a school-sponsored blog may not be supportive or reflective of the district. Accepting some entries and suppressing others for the public to see have the cause of several lawsuits protesting the violation of First Amendment rights.

DEVELOPING ACCEPTABLE
USE POLICIES (AUPs)

In the article "Acceptable Use Policies in School Districts, Myth or Reality?" by Taylor, Whang, and Tettegah (2006), AUPs are defined as "strategies that allow school districts to notify technology users of expected behavior and set for the consequences of misuse" (p. 116). Taylor et al.'s inquiry focuses on the implementation of acceptable use documents in schools, and highlight a very interesting dichotomy: Is an acceptable use document simply part of the student handbook that contains multiple documents, or is the AUP a separate document that both parents and students (and sometimes teachers) sign? This is the subject of ongoing debates within and among districts and will need to be resolved in your district, too.

Acceptable use agreements should also include a standard phrase that describes the school system's response to an AUP violation. State or federal laws can be quoted along with local school board policies or procedures. One note of importance here: School districts need to follow their disciplinary actions consistently to be defensible in court. Make sure that administrators and teachers know how to handle AUP violations through professional learning and staff development.

One of the major challenges with the legal system and AUPs is the recent evolution of these documents in an educational environment. The Children's Online Privacy Protection Act (COPPA) was originally enacted in October 1998 by Congress as an attempt to protect children when using the Internet. Unfortunately, the act itself was brought before the Supreme Court several times due to a series of challenges, each one identifying another gap in the ability of the law to sanction appropriate use of the Internet. For examples of the legal challenges, see ACLU versus Reno, ACLU versus Ashcroft and ACLU versus Gonzales. The challenge with any such law is the local definitions of what constitutes decent or appropriate uses of technology resources. Eventually, the Supreme Court deemed COPPA itself unconstitutional on the grounds that community definitions and standards could be upheld effectively by methods other than the law, and that the regional definitions of obscenity must be part of the discussion, making it impossible for courts to uphold.

- *Student AUPs.* The least arguable document, the AUP signed by the student is a simple contract between the school and student. In its simplest form, the document states that school technology will be used for teaching and learning only. Legally, however, there are many other components of an AUP but the basic idea is that technology access was purchased by the school or district for the purposes of teaching and learning or the administration of teaching and learning. This means that students will *not* use technology to harass other students, commit crimes, or use technology unethically. In *The Internet and the Law: What Educators Need to Know* by Conn (2002), several concepts are recommended for inclusion in student AUPs:

- o Computing facilities will be used exclusively for educational purposes
- o Students and teachers will use educationally appropriate speech and expression when using the Internet
- o Users' responsibilities to avoid copyright violations
- o Users' reasonable expectations of privacy
- o Users' responsibilities to avoid substantial and material disruption of the educational process for the school community

Should the AUP be a document that is signed for as part of a larger packet, a button clicked to accept access to the Internet, or an individual document for parents and students to sign and return to the school? Depending on your district's philosophy, one of these approaches is probably already being followed. The first two approaches—having a single signature for a packet of materials and clicking "I agree" to a set of standards—will probably receive the most challenges in the courtroom. If the materials were not carefully explained to every parent and a signature obtained after discussion of the documents, then a parent can legitimately claim that he or she did not know what was being signed. Clicking "I agree" or "I accept" to a list of AUP-type statements prior to accessing the Internet may also be something a student can challenge as not being explained clearly to the student. On the other hand, having an AUP signed annually by students and parents serves to refresh the students' memories of what is expected in terms of acceptable technology use, and parents will probably read through the document more clearly if it is a single document brought home by their children. The best approach is probably a combination of all three so that a parent has a reference copy of the AUP in the student handbook, the student sees a visual reminder each time he or she logs into the network, and the parent and student can discuss the AUP at the time of a signature.

• *Staff AUPs.* Many schools and districts neglect the design of a staff AUP, claiming that other school policies and procedures cover the ethical use of technology. This may be true, but there are teachers dismissed due to inappropriate technology use reported in papers all over the country on regular basis. Much like a student AUP, a staff AUP also includes a component about the protection of student data and use of professional ethics:

- o Computing facilities will be used exclusively for educational purposes
- o Students and teachers will use educationally appropriate speech and expression when using the Internet
- o Users' responsibilities to avoid copyright violations
- o Users' reasonable expectations of privacy
- o Users' responsibilities to avoid substantial and material disruption of the educational process for the school community

o Professionally derived data and information will be protected and maintained in accordance with FERPA guidelines
o Staff use of technology will conform to ethical guidelines set forth by the state's standards commission

* *Technology Team AUPs.* If staff AUPs are a rare animal, then technology team AUPs are almost an endangered species. These valuable team members have "the keys to the kingdom," so to speak, and should be held accountable for their increased access to technology resources. Passwords and access to sensitive information is part of the technology team's job, and technology team members' ethical responsibilities may be higher due to their role in the school or district.

o Computing facilities will be used exclusively for educational purposes
o Students and teachers will use educationally appropriate speech and expression when using the Internet
o Users' responsibilities to avoid copyright violations
o Users' reasonable expectations of privacy
o Users' responsibilities to avoid substantial and material disruption of the educational process for the school community
o Professionally derived data and information will be protected and maintained in accordance with FERPA guidelines
o Staff use of technology will conform to ethical guidelines set forth by the state's standards commission
o Users' responsibility to protect and maintain others' resources through appropriate safety and security measures

USING PASSWORDS TO SECURE ACCESS

In most online environments, passwords are employed to ensure data confidentiality. Most districts have chosen unique user names and passwords as the primary mechanism to restrict access to data and electronic resources, including computer- and phone-based communication tools. Proper authentication and authorization should be used at all times. This may include the required entry of a unique username and password (for example, SASI), a stored username and required password entry (such as Lotus Notes), or an enterprisewide security subsystem (such as a single sign-on mechanism to which the individual applications interface).

Passwords should be entered each time the application is started and following a period of inactivity. Many technology standards recommend a maximum of 30 minutes of inactivity before the user is prompted to reenter a password to continue working in that application or view data. The goal is to protect private data from unauthorized use, and this is especially critical when a computer workstation is located in a classroom or in public area, such as a teacher workroom.

Here are some additional guidelines for the development of password-related policies:

- Users need to be responsible for their own account information, username, and password
- Users are responsible for the activities performed under their usernames and passwords
- Users should not leave their workstation unattended
- Users should not leave information printed out or on-screen for others to see
- Users with supervisory or management responsibility for a system— such system-level or administrative computer access should not be used for regular work, but only to perform administrative duties to avoid creating a security risk for the network
- Users should not display user names and passwords on or near the computer monitor
- Users should not save district data on a nondistrict-purchased device

SUMMARY

Technology access is becoming one of the "hot buttons" of school technology. With dozens of tools and applications available to each staff members, students, and administrators, schools and districts strive to develop more simplified "collections" of resources for different groups. Whether access is designated for e-mail, the Internet, administrative tools, or instructional software management, schools should think carefully about who gets access to which resource. To make matters even more complicated, there are unique applications, such as portals, that serve as a single location for a number of resources. To help inform and manage the use of school district resources, schools typically implement an AUP. These documents serve several purposes, including reminding staff and students on an annual basis of guidelines for appropriate use. Finally, it is also important to help users develop strong passwords to protect their access to teaching and learning resources, ensuring the validity of students logging into the resources.

REFERENCES

Conn, K. (2002). *The Internet and the law: What educators need to know.* Alexandria, VA: ASCD.

Stuve, M. J. (2006). Pursuing professional identities in a digital domain. *Technology and Education, 8,* 57–70.

Wallace, M., & Webber, L. (2008). *IT governance policies and procedures: Tools and techniques that work.* New York: Aspen

Whang, E. W., & Tettegah, S. Y. (2006). Acceptable use policies in school districts: myth or reality? *Technology and Education, 8,* 115–123.

6

Buttons, Bells, and Flashing Lights

Managing K–12 Internet Use

Critical Chapter Questions

- How is the Internet being used—and misused—for instruction?
- How can policies and procedures support instructional Internet use?
- What rights do students, parents, and staff members have regarding Web use?

Chapter Focus: *Policies can support instructional Internet use while discouraging less valuable uses.*

❖

Brian is embedded in the Internet, even at school. As a sophomore in high school, he has seen and used the Internet as it grew and changed as a learning tool. Before he arrived at school, his entrance and exit onto and off of the bus was monitored by a fob attached to his backpack. As he got off the bus, the information was downloaded wirelessly to a school server, transmitted to the central office, and made available for review by his parents at work via a parent information portal. Brian walks through several halls on his way to homeroom in the morning and notes that several teachers are working on their computers, researching topics for upcoming lessons. In homeroom, his attendance data is transmitted to the parent information portal, which also contains grading information for each of his six classes. In his favorite class, sociology, Brian recently completed a research project on island communities, culminating in a mixed-media presentation of photographs, music, and statistics garnered from several online research tools purchased by the district. At lunch, his food choices in the cafeteria are transmitted to a school nutrition application, which automatically sends out inventory requests to replace the food being consumed from food vendors. When Brian steps back on the bus in the afternoon—again, being tracked, he is pleasantly surprised that his cell phone, also Wi-Fi enabled, can now connect to a new service on the bus itself: wireless access for the ride home. Brian uses his student information portal access to his teachers' Web pages and begins thinking about several projects that are due in the next few days. When Brian steps off the bus near his home, he has spent another day connected to the Internet, whether he knew it or not.

❖

Throughout our discussion on the use of technology in the classroom, the Internet has been mentioned as a peripheral component. In this chapter, we will focus more deeply on the Internet as a tool for teaching and learning, along with methods and techniques for using the Internet more safely and effectively.

Consider, for a moment, the number of places within a school where Internet services can be provided. Some schools have student workstations in every classroom, multiple computer labs, and a well-apportioned media center. Many students also have Internet-capable cell phones, bringing various versions of Internet browsers into the school during the day. There are also other types of handheld devices, from handheld productivity tools, media-playing equipment such as MP3 players and iPods, to electronic book readers such as the Amazon Kindle that can access the Internet via a variety of wireless connections.

Consider another study completed by D'Elia Abbas, Bishop, Jacobs, and Rodger (2007), "The Impact of Youth's Use of the Internet on Their Use of the Public Library." In their article, D'Elia et al. documented an interesting consideration: Do students who have the Internet at home visit the library more or less than those who do not? In a larger sense, this question is important because students have, in the past, used the library as a source for noninstructional content. While much of the library would qualify as noninstructional, there is certainly a scholastic component to library use. Most libraries now have networked computers and the Internet alone is one of the reasons to visit the library. A growing number of community libraries are also providing wireless access to the Internet, which is also a reason for visiting the library, as many homes have laptops with wireless capabilities. The study found that while students who had Internet services at home visited the community library less, the students who did not have home Internet services were more frequent visitors to the library for both instructional and noninstructional purposes.

Scholastic Internet users are becoming more and more prevalent, if the study is looked at in a different light. Where students would, in the past, have to visit the community library to find information for homework assignments and projects, they can now use the Internet as a primary resource and continue to use the Internet as a noninstructional resource, too.

INTERNET APPLICATIONS
IN THE CLASSROOM

Unlike using the Internet for business, taking advantage of all the World Wide Web has to offer can be difficult in a classroom without the right policies, procedures, and mindset for administrators, teachers, and students. In Jonathan Hart's (2008) text, *Internet Law: A Field Guide,* case after case is illuminated for being focused on the types of content available. The concepts of copyright, data collection, privacy rights, and freedom of speech have all taken on new meanings and new interpretations, and this is even more emphasized in the scholastic environment. In 2003, several music-producing companies began moving against university students for stealing, pirating, and illegally distributing music via school technology resources. Of course, this kind of infringement on the rights of music producers does not stop with just the universities because copyright violations are a common behavior among K–12 students, too.

Having a restrictive network may not be the only answer either. Richard Ferdig's (2007) article, "When 'Acceptable' becomes Unacceptable," makes a strong case for thinking clearly through the different uses of the Internet for valid instruction. A problem that arises as new Internet technologies arrive is the handling of online learning. As the definition of online learning changes, so must the policies governing online activities. "The growth of online learning has required districts to constantly reevaluate their acceptable use policies as forward-thinking educators are putting new technologies to the service of innovative teaching and learning" (Ferdig, 2007, p. 26). He recommends a sharp review of acceptable use policies (AUPs) and other documents that incorporate online learning and online collaboration tools being used by the school and district.

The Internet's explosive growth leads to a system development model first used for evolutionary theories, called the punctuated equilibrium model. First defined by paleontologists Niles Eldredge and Stephen Jay Gould in 1972, a punctuated equilibrium consists of periods of massive evolutionary change—the punctuation—followed by relatively long periods of stability while different organisms either die off or persevere—the equilibrium. The Internet follows the same model in many ways, although the timeline is months and years instead of geological time. A new Internet capability is obtained due to system improvements in processors and other computer capabilities, and a "branch" of Internet applications becomes dozens of companies trying to fill the same market niche. After a few months (or years), the successful competitors survive as market leaders in that area until the next new Internet capability arrives. Consider the history of blogging, photo sharing, social networks, and video streaming—they all followed the punctuated equilibrium model.

Just like animals that go extinct, Internet application providers disappear or are subsumed into larger companies, making it extremely difficult to plan long-range strategies for Internet use. Applications that meet district needs today may not be available next month or next year. Policies and procedures that are crafted with Internet applications in mind may need to be revised regularly to meet the needs of a changing application environment.

Instructional Focus Areas

The Internet is, among other things, a tremendous resource for instruction, providing everything from online content to specialized, streamed programming that is broadcast live to a classroom. Instructional Web-based applications come in an amazing variety of costs, content, distribution models, applicability, grade levels, and delivery mechanisms. The challenge with the variety of combinations used by vendors and free providers is the creation of policies and procedures that are flexible enough to address appropriate teaching and learning needs. To add to this potential confusion, there is a new development, Internet2, which is high-quality, high-interactivity Internet access. In an article by Stuart Nachbar (2007), he notes that like the original Internet, Internet2 relies on the active involvement of research universities to develop, implement, and maintain the network; but unlike the Internet, Internet2's academic and instructional uses go far beyond scientific research at the doctoral level into national and sometimes global programs that are presented in K–12 classrooms through interactive videoconferencing. K–12 schools can both create and deliver programming through Internet2 or purchase programming from a content provider, such as a college or university, museum, library, or performing arts center.

Changes in Internet-delivered content do not stop with Internet2 however. Vendors are identifying new ways to put content in the hands of teachers and students, using everything from handheld computing devices to tablet computers to innovative interactive technology. Internet-based instructional applications can be used to diagnose learning deficiencies in both content and cognition, connect students to tutors or other students, and provide a wealth of multimedia resources for lesson development. As a result, policies must accommodate equipment and technology advances that are currently only in the "dream" stage.

If you have been in the classroom for several years, you might be acutely aware of how much of the curriculum is driven by textbook adoptions. Textbooks were the curriculum, and the curriculum was based on the textbooks and related publisher-driven resources. Teachers typically had a great deal of autonomy in the development of specific lessons, but there was a limited range of content availability for any given subject and grade level. With the use of the Internet as a content resource, however, teachers and students have a new level of control for their classroom content. Additionally, students may be able to drive their own learning experiences, making the learning both differentiated for the student and more actuated if they are more deeply engaged in the learning process.

However, for curriculum planners, Internet content may also be a double-edged sword. Without appropriate review processes to evaluate the content in a meaningful way against specific learning standards, teachers and students run the risk of using inappropriate, inconsistent, or incorrect information. As noted by David Zandvliet and Leon Straker (2001) in their article, "Physical and Psychosocial Aspects of the Learning Environment in Information Technology Rich Classrooms," the role of the teacher takes on a different aspect. They acknowledge that "the successful use of computers means involving students and educators in the learning process in new ways. As with any medium, the vitality of computer use in schools depends on good teaching. Professional knowledge about student learning, curricula and classroom organization should complement other important information on effective, product, and safe computer use by children" (p. 839). The teacher's role in the classroom is just as interactive but has a new aspect of technology awareness that serves the students in the learning process.

Since finding the right content is a challenge for many schools and teachers, many states have developed significant curriculum resources to guide teachers and students in the direction of high-quality, online learning tools. While not a robust learning management system or online learning delivery system, these tools can be powerful learning supplements for teachers, department chairs, and curriculum leaders at all grade levels. For example, the state of Georgia's department of education has developed a free, public Web site that provides information and resources to help meet the educational needs of students through the Georgia Performance Standards in three different categories of foci: teachers, administrators, and parents (see http://www.georgiastandards.org). In Ohio, curriculum resources are available under Learning Supports, and the section includes both curriculum and administrative resources (see http://www.ohiorc .org/standards/ohio for more information).

Policies and procedures developed for instructional, Internet-delivered instructional resources must be designed as flexible, "living" documents that bend (but hopefully do not break) with the instructional needs of both students and teachers.

Noninstruction Focus Areas

While instructional applications are the bread and butter of school technology, the number of noninstructional, Internet-based applications is growing on a daily basis. From securing teacher and student access to computer to keeping the school nutrition inventory ordering process moving smoothly, there seems to be an application for just about every aspect of school technology. The question for noninstructional Internet use then becomes, can this be clearly connected to teaching and learning, or support of teaching and learning?

Examples of engaging the Internet to accomplish the support activities in a school district are easy to find. In an article by Rama Ramaswami (2007), "The X Files," Colorado's Adams County School District 50 is noted as being a leader in the development of unique Internet-based, noninstructional applications. Wireless access is being used for "doors, alarms, IDs—we've even thought of putting a few access points in the parking lot," the technology systems administrator for the district noted (p. 24). Ramaswami (2007) explains that the pervasive Internet raises privacy concerns, but the trade-off benefit is one of being able to manage the responsible for hundreds or thousands of students throughout the school day.

Policies that address noninstructional Internet use will probably devote some attention on student data protection. Children's Internet Protection Act (CIPA) and Family Educational Rights and Privacy Act (FERPA) govern conceptual guidelines, making the accidental or inappropriate divulgence of student information a serious concern for school districts. This has become a significant concern for many users of the Internet, not just students, and a number of states have even created additional legislation to protect their residents. California created an Online Privacy Protection Act, New York enacted a law requiring state agencies to develop online privacy policies, and Nebraska, Pennsylvania, and other states have laws that specify that making false or misleading statements in a privacy policy is a prohibited deceptive business practice (Hart, 2008). As extensions of state agencies, schools and districts should also be prepared to offer solid assurances for the protection of data backed up by effective business decisions to protect student and staff information.

Another noninstructional use of the Internet should also be considered: student creation of content and criticism of schools, teachers, and other students. How will the school or district react to students posting inappropriate content, hateful content, or subversive content with their home computers, especially when such content creates difficulties in the classroom environment? A number of legal cases have addressed the concerns of schools, districts, and students in this area: J.S. versus Bethlehem Area School District; Emmett versus Kent School District No. 415; In re I.M.L, a minor versus State of Utah; Dwyer v. Oceanport School District; Goldsmith versus Gwinnett County School District; and J.S. versus Blue Mountain School District, to identify just a few. In most cases, the courts drew a clear distinction between what happened on campus and what was done off campus, as well as the disruptions caused in the teaching and learning process because of the Internet activity. For example, in Requa versus Kent School District, a student was accused of filming his teachers surreptitiously at school then editing the video clips at home to include students making lewd gestures of students behind the teachers' backs. The school district's disciplinary action was upheld because of the on-campus filming activities, not the off-campus editing of the footage at the student's home.

This brings up another important point. Policies can only go so far in the school environment. Once students leave the building or learning environment, their behaviors can cause more than a policy violation, and can even become legal events. Students now have the ability to film someone with their camera phones and upload it immediately to the Internet, whether or not the receiving Internet site is blocked by the school district. Are there policies in place for your district or school that address these kinds of behaviors?

School and Teacher Web Sites

A corollary activity to school-related Internet-based activities is the development of school and teacher Web sites to provide everything from weekly newsletters to classroom announcements to homework assignments. School Web sites can also be the quick "go to" resource for parents trying to find out if the school is closed in inclement weather, find the first name or e-mail of a specific teacher, or to see what supplies their child should bring on the first day of school. Unfortunately, many school Web sites tend to be disorganized visual messes: links are inconsistent, pages are filled with graphically flashy but cognitively disruptive images, and students' photographs are displayed without regard to student privacy regulations. Some school Web sites carry advertisements, provide links to nondistrict entities like booster clubs and still more hide links behind menu bars that not user-friendly.

Teachers are using the Internet more frequently as a communications tool to augment classroom activities, and, while many are doing this well, quite a few still need some help in Web site development and management. Ideally, a teacher's Web site should either provide timely information, such as daily updates or assignments, or provide relevant information, such as the course syllabus or parent-related information. Many teacher Web sites are incomplete and represent the teacher (and school) poorly due to grammar errors, incomplete content, and unclear information.

For both school and teacher Web sites, a set of policies and procedures should be developed to protect student identity and ensure appropriate, reliable information broadcast about the school, the district, or the teacher. In an article by Miller, Adsit, and Miller (2005) suggest formal creation of content for a Web site are discussed. Mission statements; rules and policies; teacher information; school news; cafeteria menus; links for teachers, parents, and students; and the school's Internet use policy were all part of the review of 70 elementary school Web sites. Combined with a survey on the importance of a number of components for parents, students, and teachers, this research notes the gap between what is desired for school Web pages and what is actually on the school Web pages (Miller et al., 2005). Your school or district may want to conduct a similar study based on your current Web page.

Social Networking Sites

School use of social networking sites has been met with a range of responses, from an enthusiastic cheer on the part of students and teachers to a frostily disdainful frown. The largest challenge with any social networking technology not specifically designed for education, including blogs, wikis, contact databases, and more robust networking sites like Facebook and MySpace, is the inability to manage content before it reaches students. This is not a new challenge, but social networking lends itself to "anonymous communications" that include bullying, slander, and harassment.

Some schools and teachers try to use social networking resources to keep students connected to school activities and events, and to provide school and classroom news in a streamlined manner. However, if the school district does not own and manage the resource, other information, such as advertisements, solicitations, and unauthorized communications, can move into the "student space." Additionally, communications among students and parents become unregulated as well, and there are several cases in court at the time of this writing where parents have harassed students via social networking sites.

In Aimée Bissonette's (2009) book, *Cyber Law: Maximizing Safety and Minimizing Risk in Classrooms,* she outlines a number of guidelines that quickly adapt to strong policy development, including the policy components to define limited forum capabilities use in the district, such as with an online campus, and policies regarding off-campus speech of teachers and staff. Policies in this area are fairly new, since social networking is not currently well defined. Schools and districts that want to stay ahead of the students, however, should pay attention to this area of policy development.

School-related court cases are still emerging, and there is no clear process for predicting a ruling in lawsuits. The reason for differing court cases goes back to the impact on teaching and learning. Harassment, which is defined, in part, as creating a hostile work environment, can certainly be witnessed in bullying situations. Harassment that occurs off campus becomes a school problem when it impacts teaching and learning, which is hard to prove except in the most severe cases. As a result, the courts have struggled to define where the school's authority lies in such cases.

POLICY DEVELOPMENT TO SUPPORT INSTRUCTIONAL INTERNET USE

As school-based Internet use becomes more prevalent, developing appropriate policies and procedures becomes more difficult. Building flexibility into the policies to accommodate emerging Internet users can be summarized briefly as a question: Is this Internet activity for the purposes of teaching and learning or the support of teaching and learning? Unfortunately, there is a corollary: Will this work with our current technology while promoting teaching and learning or the support of teaching and learning?

Web Filtering

CIPA requires Web filtering on computers where students will be accessing resources, especially the Internet. There are typically two methods for filtering Web sites. In Web-address-based filtering, each requested Web address or link is reviewed against a *white list* or a *black list* to make sure the Web site is appropriate. This usually requires the purchase of a service that compiles such lists. A second method of filtering is based on the page content, scanning each word and metatag for inappropriate words, phrases, and content. Many schools use a combination of both types of blocking to accomplish their school Internet filtering. As a result, school districts must declare that they have a filtering system, and many districts include the phrase, "to the extent practicable," since there is always the risk of something inappropriate finding its way onto the screen.

Another connection to create in your school or district's policies or procedures is a clear line between CIPA, any of your state's laws on CIPA, and your board's Internet filtering policies. Some schools choose to create levels of blocking, giving different levels of filtering service to students, teachers, administrators, and technology team members, and that should be spelled out in the policies, too. Finally, try to avoid finite, limiting terms, like *all*, *never*, *every*, and *always*, since there may be unforeseen circumstances that the policy needs to accommodate.

Effective Instructional Web Use Guidelines

Policies for scholastic Internet use should be designed with broad usage of the learning resources as possible. Depending on the classroom, the school, and the district, different philosophies will have to be built into the policy. Is your school or district restrictive? Are there a plethora of resources already purchased by the district for student and staff member use? Has your school or district purchased special prefiltered Internet connections designed with learners in mind, such as Nettrekker or AskForKids.com? If so, then consider including the "predefined search resources" in your policies and procedures as the mandatory starting point for all students.

Another component of policies regarding learning-focused Internet use should be management of student information posted on the Web. Student privacy, protection of images and work, and even media release forms should be readily available on the school Web site, with a link to, or directions to access, the policies and procedures as well. Performance scores, such as school test reports or assessment summaries, should never be publicly available in a disaggregated format. Finally, reviewing school and teacher Web sites on an annual basis to ensure compliance is a solid standard and a useful practice to include in policies and procedures.

Provisions for User Activity Audits

Speaking of reviewing school and teacher Web sites, there is another area of policies for review: IT audits. Since many technology policies clearly state that technology can be audited for use at any time, it is helpful to detail some procedures around such an audit (Wallace & Webber, 2006). If audits or reviews are not specifically included in the instructional technology policies, the school or district may not have a strong footing for conducting audits at all.

Audits can be completed on a routine basis but may be limited to certain systems or activities. For example, some companies regularly audit e-mails, looking for specific keywords that are outside of the realm of acceptable use. School districts focused on maintaining standardized support models might audit computers for hardware and software changes, identifying software that is inappropriately installed on computers. Still other districts might perform an IT audit to identify potential changes in the software packages installed on school computers.

Throughout the audit process, a high degree of professional privacy must be maintained, which is why many companies and districts hire external vendors to complete audits. Be aware of your legal rights where audits are concerned and make sure that policies are reviewed by your legal groups prior to implementing. Yes, there may be laws that prohibit the use of technology for nonteaching-and-nonlearning purposes but that varies from state to state. Instead, work to make your district's policies a clear indicator of what to expect in terms of hardware and software reviews and audits. The best policy in this area is one that is well communicated out to the technology users on a regular basis.

Collaborative Learning Environments

The collaborative work environment is one of the most difficult areas of emerging technology to manage with policies and procedures. Perhaps the challenge is due to the uniqueness of technology-moderated collaboration, perhaps the difficulty arises from the number of students involved, but it might just be the reality that, without proper guidance, teachers and students are not aware of the boundaries for learning collaboration. Learning environment collaboration is no longer just pen pals from overseas.

The modern face of collaboration occurs in a technology-moderated environment across the world and across the school district. In many cases, collaborative technology is being used to extend the curriculum offerings of regular schools, providing college-level coursework for advanced or special-project students. This can occur in both large- and small-scale projects, and one of the latest evolutions of the collaborative classroom is the digital field trip. Many science educators remember the groundbreaking work of the JASON project, where live oceanographic data was transmitted to classrooms courtesy of the National Geographic Society and Dr. Robert Ballard in 1989. The timing was right for this project because the technology was finally in place for such a massive collaborative undertaking.

Collaboration requires a special set of policies, since not every person involved may be a student or an employee of your school or district. Instead, policies should focus on the *intent* of the collaborative activity, making the collaboration process appropriate for teaching and learning, regardless of the participants. For example, policies may require parents to agree to allow their students to communicate with different groups in other school systems. Parents should be aware that not all communications are monitored and controlled by teachers and that each student's behavior will be graded as part of the learning process. Teachers also need to give a great deal of thought to protecting student identities, assigning students into groups for collaborative activities, and spending quite a bit of time preparing and monitoring the learning activities.

Communicating Beyond the Learning Environment

As an extension of collaborative learning environments, moving your classroom to a "location" where it will interact with adults in specific fields as part of scholastic event sounds quite a bit like Scholastic's *The Magic School Bus*. However, these types of events, where students are at work sites, research centers, and universities around the world, are becoming more and more common. Here policies have a different meaning, because you, as a teacher or administrator, may have absolutely no control over the communications among students and teachers. With many of these types of learning activities, the organizers understand the need to protect students but occasionally inappropriate comments or questions occur.

Much like other collaborative learning environments, the key is to inform parents, invite them to be part of the process, and teach the students to be mindful of appropriate behaviors throughout events. Release forms, alternative materials, and administrative involvement should also be part of the policies and procedures around collaborative learning. Typically a little planning for collaborative events and the protection of students goes a long way if there is inappropriate behavior during the use of collaborative technology.

POLICIES TO PROTECT OTHERS' PRIVACY AND PERSONAL RIGHTS

In many collaborative or technology-moderated learning events, one of the common challenges is keeping confidentiality throughout the collaborative events. Due to a variety of confidentiality breaches, many teachers and administrators are already sensitive to data confidentiality topics, but online pen pals, study groups, field trips, and collaborative workspaces like blogs and wikis open students up to a whole new range of exposure. From sharing of e-mails to cyber bullying, online environments require a sharp eye on privacy and personal rights, whether the participants are students, staff members, or community members.

As mentioned in previous chapters, while directory information is public information, it is only public in the sense that it can be requested and that it is distributed through official paths to approved parties. Personnel information, on the other hand, remains very much in a gray zone because adults in the school system have different rights than students. Families and community members in the school society are another gray area. After all, if the community member's information can be found in a phone book, why would a school protect that information when they are helping a teacher on a real-world classroom project? There is very little legal precedence to protect anything other than student data, but it's only a matter of time before school districts must be aware of their responsibilities to the community.

Students

There are, of course, a number of laws protecting the identity and work products of students. From test scores to film clips, and from class schedules to media center records, schools have become experts at keeping student records safe. However, the policies at the school or district that support student data protection will also need to be regularly visited and updated. Specifically, the items to review are components of directory information, parental and community rights to information in your state, and what data your school or district collects. Additionally, if your school has a parent information portal, your policies and procedures should reflect parental access to school or district resources, and parents should have some agreement that they physically or electronically sign to gain access to their students' records. Secondarily, if the parent signs for access electronically, how is the district or school ensuring correct identity prior to granting access? This should be included in the policy as well.

When designing policies, keep in mind that policies should shape appropriate culture of data protection overall. For example, teachers should be trained to protect printouts, student progress reports, and student work examples as confidential information when not on campus. Keeping individual student information safe is a professional behavior that teachers often already use but formalizing such behaviors into policies and procedures protects the schools and the teachers.

Staff Members

The concept of protecting staff member data from electronic exploitation is somewhat new since the focus has been on managing student data for so long. Human resource data has become enmeshed in many districts' financial applications and data warehouses. However, unlike student data, adult data can be used more readily for credit fraud and more malicious purposes if data is exploited. For a real eye-opening list of school districts that have suffered data breaches of personnel information, use the keywords "school district data breach" in your search engine.

How do information breaches occur now that the majority of personnel information is maintained electronically? You might be surprised to know that hacking is only a small portion of staff data exposure. The majority is from the theft of data-rich equipment, like laptops, hard drives, and computer systems. A few involve the misuse of paper documents. While social security numbers are not printed on as many documents as in the past, the use of social security information inappropriately has become a significant black-market activity.

Policies that will help the protection of staff data will also hinge on a culture of data protection, not just a single policy available to the employees. Conveniently, the newspapers provide plenty of frightening examples of data theft to inform your staff members. However, policies in this area should detail what kinds of documents actually contain sensitive information and what measures are taken to protect such data. Employees in the human resources or records groups may also be provided with extra training to help them understand the risks involved. Additionally, any contractors working in your departments should systematically remove personnel data from their computers periodically, which is the cause of a surprisingly large number of public sector data breaches.

Parents and Community Members

The final group that needs additional protection through policies and procedures is the public-at-large group of parents and community members. While not specifically targeted by the school district's policies and procedures, parents and community members are often at the school for various functions. For examples, students and parents are photographed for an upcoming newsletter. If the school or district does not inform parents that their images may be used for school publications, then the district or school may find itself in the midst of some difficult discussions. Community members involved in work-study programs may also find their work or images used in scholastic publications, and a media release form would also be a wise item to obtain prior to distribution.

In many cases, policies around the protection of community members' personal rights are simple yet effective. Such a media release form may simply state that the community member agrees to have their image, picture, or work products displayed by the school in a manner supporting teaching and learning. The same goes for parents, but FERPA considerations imply that the school or district work toward informing parents more thoroughly. Regular communications to parents that note the use of parent and family images during school functions may be published by the school would be a positive trust-building discussion that the school could have. After all, if the parents are consistently reminded that data is carefully managed, they are more likely to trust the overall data management processes throughout the school or district.

SUMMARY

As a teaching and learning tool, the Internet has changed the face of education, the classroom, and even the interactions among teachers, students, parents, and administrators. With both positive and negative ramifications, Internet resources are used to provide instruction applications, noninstruction content, public "pictures" of teachers, schools, and districts through Web pages, and even communities through social networking. On the positive side, there are many useful free and for-purchase services that assist in education. On the negative side, there is so much information on the Internet that students, teachers, and parents can get confused or view inappropriate information when using the Web. Policies help clarify appropriate use within the school context, but also set the tone for at-home use of school-purchased Internet-based tools. Another component of Internet use is the collaborative nature of the Web, and policies protect students when using interactive communication tools like blogs, wikis, and virtual environments. Ultimately, instructional technology policies and procedures protect the privacy and personal rights of school personnel and students using the Internet for teaching and learning or the support of teaching and learning.

REFERENCES

Bissonette, A. M. (2009). *Cyber law: Maximizing safety and minimizing risk in classrooms.* Thousand Oaks, CA: Corwin.

D'Elia, G., Abbas, J., Bishop, K., Jacobs, D., & Rodger, E. J. (2007). The impact of youth's use of the Internet on their use of the public library. *Journal of the American Society for Information Science and Technology, 581*(14), 2180–2196.

Ferdig, R. E. (2007). When "acceptable" becomes unacceptable. *T H E Journal, 34*(12), 26–27.

Hart, J. D. (2008). *Internet law: A field guide* (6th ed.). Arlington, VA: BNA Books.

Miller, S., Adsit, K. I., & Miller, T. (2005). Evaluating the importance of common components in school-based Web sites: Frequency of appearance and stakeholders' judged value. *TechTrends: Linking Research and Practice to Improving Learning, 49*(6), 34–40.

Nachbar, S. (2007, April). The Internet's second coming. *T H E Journal, 34*(4), 46–48.

Ramaswami, R. (2007, September). The X files. *T H E Journal, 34*(9), 24–28.

Wallace, M., & Webber, L. (2006). *IT policies and procedures, 2007 Edition (IT Policies & Procedures Manual)* (2007 ed.). New York: Aspen.

Zandvliet, D. B., & Straker, L. M. (2001). Physical and psychosocial aspects of the learning environment in information technology rich classrooms. *Ergonomics, 44*(9), 858–857.

7

No Stone Unturned

*Implementing Technology
Policies and Procedures*

Critical Chapter Questions

- How can the school culture be changed to support policy compliance?
- What is the role of technology team members in the implementation of technology policies?
- How can parents and community members support policy compliance?

Chapter Focus: *Determine the most appropriate methods for successfully implementing technology policies and procedures.*

❖

As a middle school administrator, Hector feels like the central offices have lost their collective minds. After bringing an expert in for several days, the district has rolled out a small flotilla of new policies, many of which are around instructional technology. Hector knows that the policies have a good point—to protect students—but feels like focusing on this initiative is just one more straw on the camel's back. As the administrator in charge of curriculum and technology in his school, Hector wonders how in the world he will get his teachers to change their practices midway through the year.

Of course, policies and procedures had been discussed as part of his leadership degree programs. The need for policies and procedures is clear, but the implementation of policies in a school or district was never discussed. His coursework even included information on how to create effective policies and procedures. Instead, professors and colleagues seemed to assume that everyone already had a full complement of policies and that schools and districts already operated within the policies in an effective manner. If a rule specified in a policy was broken, there were punitive actions that could be taken. If someone requested policies for review, Hector knew the guidelines for providing those policies and procedures. However, he was at a serious loss when it came to turning those policies into actionable behaviors in staff members.

Worse yet, Hector's two-person technology staff would be restricted in their actions due to these board-mandated policy changes. The technology staff, consisting of one lab manager and one technician, was already quite frazzled in the care of 2,000 students and 150 teachers. Hector knew that they would each need to take a leadership role in the implementation process but was concerned that this might be seen as negative if the technology staff members really spoke their minds. When Hector's school was given their annual audit by the district's school improvement team in three months, right before school ended, they would expect to see some improvement. What could he accomplish by then?

EXPLORING THE IMPACT OF POLICIES ON THE LEARNING CULTURE

It sounds familiar, doesn't it? There is *always* too much to do and too little time to accomplish anything meaningful. However, we, as professionals, continue to do what we can in our (hopefully) positive impact of teaching and learning. Policies and procedures, which may seem like about the most trivial of all of the central office or district functions, tend to carry a disproportional amount of weight when lawyers, auditors, and newspaper reporters are involved. When calamity knocks on the school or classroom door, some rarely opened binder appears in the hands of a school district official, and policies and procedures are viewed as the antithesis to getting the job of teaching and learning with students.

The Truth Could Not Be More Different

If policies and procedures are written and maintained appropriately, they become a solid sounding board of appropriate behaviors, *especially* when there is an inflammatory event at a school. In Nancy Campbell's (1998) excellent text, *Writing Effective Policies and Procedures: A Step-by-Step Resource for Clear Communication,* she cautions,

> There's practical and legal danger in allowing policies and procedures to become old and faded. People begin to ignore the irrelevant

ones, and soon they're ignoring all of them. Guesswork becomes prevalent. Errors, some of them serious, start to occur. And right behind that comes legal trouble. (p. 343)

She and I both advocate a regular review of policies and procedures along with ad hoc reviews and adjustments, and a regular stream of communication to support policy and procedure use.

In the school environment, policies and procedures may receive a level of resistance if they are not implemented effectively. In the area of technology policies and procedures, incorporating policies and procedures into the daily flow of the school and district may require additional support development to make sure everyone gets the message on how the policies support teaching and learning. Regardless, the most important thing to change the school or district culture to both contribute to policies and procedures for instructional technology and work with the existing policy makers to improve existing policies.

Some guiding principles can be used with all of the approaches discussed in this chapter. First, communication is extremely important (you will hear this several more times during this discussion) and must not be neglected. Second, providing alternative resources is essential, meaning written explanations, support personnel, and open forums for discussion. Third, the review of policies and procedures must be ongoing and connected to the district's strategies for teaching, learning, personnel management, and facilities management. Hopefully, your school or district can pull from the following strategies to create a *mix* of policy support that works effectively.

Classroom Culture

The classroom typically involves two groups of people: teachers and students. The teachers need clear guidelines for their students, and the students need to understand the acceptable use policies (AUPs) so that they stay within the appropriate boundaries. One challenge with the classroom culture, though, is that the classroom computer is perceived as noninstructional in many cases. Teachers use it for "reward time" when students complete work satisfactorily, students use it as a personal e-mail resource when they can get onto the computer, and since there are not enough computers for students, students view the time as a novelty when they can actually sit at the computer.

However, classroom computers and other technology are all part of a larger strategy to provide teaching and learning experiences throughout the instructional day. While teachers understand the importance of keeping students safe while online, they rarely have the ability to pay attention to everything the student does on the computer. Typically, students try to use computers at school the way that they would use their computers at home and that is often radically different than a computer being used for teaching and learning. Policies and procedures can help guide the students' perspectives that the classroom technology should be used appropriately at all times.

Changing the classroom culture around policies and procedures can be accomplished through several activities, and these must be repeated annually if not more than once a year. A key process is to sign the AUP annually. Yearly training on appropriate technology use, along with how to avoid cyber bullying, helps steer the classroom culture in the right direction, and so does the regular review of media release forms. For teachers, training on appropriate classroom technology use can provide a forum for improving technology use by students in the classroom (Rosenfeld & Martinez-Pons, 2005).

As a result, your policies and procedures should be adjusted to recommend some of these annual activities. Mandating an annual acceptance of the AUP or media release forms, for example, are prime candidates for required activities. Policies should probably address cyber bullying education but that may need a less rigid treatment in the specific board documents. Another good idea for the implementation of policies and procedures is to produce systemwide public service announcements describing appropriate technology use that are to be shown at faculty meetings, computer lab orientations, parent-teacher-technology nights, and other public events. This type of communication has broader appeal and may reach audiences differently than paper-based documents distributed to parents during the school's open house night.

School Culture

Another activity to support teacher technology implementation and understanding is to provide ongoing staff development throughout the school year. Whether the training is built into a certification model, a brown-bag lunch series, or a practical hands-on technology task training, ongoing staff development is a key component for technology acculturation. Teacher training can be accomplished by grade or ability level, by topic or interest, or by location in the school building. As long as teachers are taking technology training, they are more likely to implement effective technology use in the classroom (Stiler, 2005).

Another way to excite teachers about the use of technology in their classrooms is to focus on emerging technologies that may be used for teaching and learning. The most effective way for this to work is if the school has grant funding or additional funding that might be useful when purchasing small quantities of new tools. The benefit with this approach is that you will have some natural "first adopters" who will become technology advocates over time, especially if the teachers take a leadership role in the evaluation of the technology for classroom use.

In the article "Child's Play," Woolsey and Woolsey (2008) write,

In the worst case [of classroom technology use], most students have no exposure to these tools and adults take little role in connecting these digital skills with classroom activities. Even when schools do engage digital technologies, they seem unable to deal with the ambiguities of the use of new media and their rapid rate of change. And so they clench onto old paradigms of computer use, even as these do not model even the patterns of today's adults, let alone the adults of a decade from now. (p. 130)

They identify a new model: teachers and students learning together, supporting one another in the exploration of digital media. "General observations of youth suggest that the digital media competencies of youth and adults are highly complementary, with youth more masterful with technical issues and adults with fundamental principles" (Woolsey & Woolsey, 2008, p. 135). Clearly the integration of technology into schools will require new models of teaching, learning, and technology incorporation.

Policies and procedures are supported with teacher-specific communications that are appropriate in faculty meetings and teacher training. If your district has multiple schools, providing training presentations or handouts with policy information is a good way for training redelivery to actually hit its mark of making teachers more aware of policies and procedures. These approaches do not have to be complex, but they must be easily understood and highly practicable. When developing policy and procedure training for teachers, keep in mind the need to relate the information immediately into the classroom.

District Culture

Paradoxically, the most difficult place to create a policy culture around technology is also the source of the policies and procedures themselves. Technology availability in the schools is often driven by district decisions as well, contributing to the use of modern resources in the classroom. However, the district has one other powerful resource that schools may not be able to bring to the table themselves: staff development on a large scale. With staff development, the district culture can be shifted through a number of policy-focused improvements, creating a stronger awareness and practical approach to the application of technology policies. As new technologies are purchased districtwide or rolled out on a limited basis, district staff development can include policy and procedure training as part of technology implementation.

The district culture also plays a key role in the motivation to use technology more appropriately. District communications and personnel development play into employees' and teachers' *technical confidence* and *confidence in approach* in the use of information technology, which is a significant component of technology adoption and policy-adhering culture (Deaney & Hennessy, 2007). The evaluation of school technology policy and procedure adoption into the classroom can also be accomplished at the district level, which would be more meaningful than a single evaluation at a school. Overall, the district, while removed from the classroom or school, is a solid resource in the acculturation of technology policies and procedures.

SHAPING THE CULTURE WITH SCHOOL TECHNOLOGY POLICIES AND PROCEDURES

School culture is typically shaped through several motivating factors, or forces. One force is the district or administrative requirements that dictate curriculum, classroom technology availability, and personnel counts. Another force is the funding structure in the district and the schools. Yet another force is the community in which the district is placed. Another force is the transience of students into and out of the school district. All of these forces either drive a culture of centralized policy compliance or a culture of individual implementation of policies in schools and classrooms. To help shape school technology cultures, the following approaches have been detailed.

System-Level Approach

The key to the system-level approach is to think through the policy development and implementation process thoroughly before rolling out any policy development or changes. If you work in a central office, inviting local school representatives to help develop strategies is critical. Additionally, involving others in the policy-development process creates "instant advocates" because the developers become the local school advocates.

Systemwide policy information can be formal and accompanied by slide shows, newsletters, regular "policy watch" e-mails from the central office, and even video messages presented at faculty meetings or PTA meetings. Conversely, policy information can also be informal, with discussion forums, breakout sessions, and panel planning teams. Regardless of the method, the key to a system-level approach for shifting culture is similar to a marketing campaign, since the strategy is to communicate and ask the recipients to do something based on their new awareness.

For example, a culture-changing strategy might be to provide a "picture" of inappropriate use, perhaps in a video format, and then follow it up with what behaviors your school or district is trying to encourage. Imagine a video of two girls bullying another classmate using school technology resources and another student realizes what they are doing. When the observing student considers a course of action, narration "explodes" her choices and suggests the best option for the student to pursue. When the video resumes, the student makes the appropriate choice and the narration concludes by a reiteration of the decision-making steps and appropriate behaviors. Perhaps it sounds too contrived, but messages like these actually do help when shaping student behaviors.

Information Dispersal Approach

Another approach is through the broad distribution of materials in a variety of pathways, adapted to multiple situations and audiences. When using information dispersal methods, the goal is to canvas the school with helpful tips and policy components whenever possible. From brochures to announcements, parent presentations to student leadership activities, from administrator training to lesson planning, policies become part of the visual and behavioral elements of the school.

This approach works best when the school or district has a strong mix of policy-supporting behaviors, staff members clearly understand the roles and intent of policies, and there are multiple opportunities for technology use for students so correct behaviors and discussions around technology use become commonplace. This strategy works best if there is a team of personnel developing new materials that can be distributed to the district or school on a regular basis.

Local Expert Approach

The third approach mentioned here is an approach that brings teachers, technologists, and students together to solve technology issues in the schools. Much like a train-the-trainer type of program, the local expert approach provides training for a number of people in the school, such as elementary grade-level chairpersons or high school department chairs. This specialized learning provides hands-on methods for supporting policy implementation, along with resources for redistributing necessary changes in the school culture for policies to be implemented. This approach works best when there is a sudden "push" to implement policies and procedures in the area of instructional technology.

For example, a summer review team is developed, composed of administrators, teachers, media specialists, school technologists, and a few parents and students. Their goal is to research the best practices for technology policies and procedures, and then suggest any changes or additions to the existing documents. The team is also asked to suggest and draft any communications that should accompany the policy improvements, taking into account the specific needs of the schools and any incidents involving technology policies and procedures during the school year. By the end of the summer, the schools can choose representatives for a broader training event, including each school and providing a full spectrum of information to be used immediately in schools.

SUPPORTING CULTURE CHANGE
WITH TECHNOLOGY TEAM MEMBERS

If your school or district is fortunate enough to have dedicated local school technology team members, part of their responsibilities includes education about technology policies and procedures. Unlike other staff members, many of these staff members fall into two categories: instructional technology support or purely technical assistance. In many cases, instructional technologists are initially teachers then take on a new job role in the schools. Remember, too, that your media specialists are part of your school technology team due to the advent of research technology and knowledge resources that are exclusively online.

Perhaps it seems like a stretch to include school technology personnel as part of your policy and procedure education. In some cases, this is due to personality conflicts and an overwhelming sense of "too much to do" in any given instructional day. That is precisely the point: There is no way to "police" everything that is done on school technology. Therefore, strong policies and procedures must be part of the culture to prevent the number of technology-related mishaps. As technology-focused personnel, technology team members have a pivotal role in the implementation of policies and procedures at the student level, too.

Educating Students and Staff in the School

Staff development, team training, peer teaching, coaching, and classroom instruction have all been used in the recent past to support technology training. It only makes sense, therefore, to follow similar models for instructional technology policy and procedure education. Policy and procedure education is best accomplished in conjunction with technology-focused learning because then the education has a cognitive connection and a strong point of reference. Having policy training just for the sake of the training may not be nearly as effective as evidenced by the number of students who, in schools around the country, are surprised when they are disciplined for using technology inappropriately even though they had signed an AUP.

Since many school technologists have a staff development role for at least a part of their responsibilities, then the face time with teachers in a development function is perfect for helping staff members learn more about policies. For example, student data reporting tools that seem to be the rage among vendors all require at least a small amount of personnel training. While this training is going on, a number of policies can be discussed such as policies protecting student and staff member data privacy, instructional ethics when using the computer, technology protection, password creation, and even laptop theft prevention.

The same is true when teaching students, and by introducing topics such as cyber bullying, the importance of an AUP, or password protection, the local school technologist can have brief but informative discussions around the district or school instructional technology policies. An important component to remember when providing instruction to students is the concept of privilege. This means that the technology is provided to help improve learning methods in the classroom, but if students do not consider the policies when using school technology, they may lose access rights or be subject to disciplinary measures. In other words, the students lose the *privilege* of using technology in their educational process.

As professional educators, many teachers still think that the only way for learning to occur is through group or individual instruction in a classroom setting. However, more and more school staff members and students are able to learn in new ways, the most powerful being a new reliance on self-teaching. Instead some school technologists have developed dynamic databases full of technology tips that can be applied to a number of situations. Ranging from slide shows to handouts to lesson ideas to links, these resources are a powerful addition to a school's instructional "arsenal." However, make sure that instructional technology policies and procedures receive a section of importance, too.

Educating the Larger School Community

In addition to educating staff members and students, the community at large also needs reassurance that students are protected through policies and procedures. The contribution of school technology team members would be perfect additions to the agenda on curriculum nights, open houses, and parent-teacher organization meetings. Some possible topics include Web site blocking, AUPs, student data protection, and appropriate use of school technology equipment. Many schools have technology nights or similar events, helping parents and community members understand how technology has improved education, and policies can be part of these gatherings.

Policies can also build a bridge between schools and businesses in the community because, as public documents, they allow businesses to contribute expertise in exchange for a stronger community. Policies set the ground rules for technology donations, online collaboration or virtual field trips to work sites, and even protect students when they are part of school-sponsored summer internships or on-the-job training programs. Without an agreement on the policies to be followed by both the school and the businesses, students may not be protected and their personal information may be compromised while off campus.

If your larger school community includes higher education institutions, don't forget to consider your policies and procedures when innovative learning programs emerge to help students earn early college credit. As a fast-growing trend (remember the punctuated equilibrium discussed earlier?), school district-university collaboration is touted as a great way to assist your high-performing students. As a result, poorly managed policies tend to fall out of date quickly, and policies and procedures designed for instructional technology are some of the first victims of such rapid change.

Since school technologists are often extremely aware of these programs, they can be on the leading edge of improving or creating policies to fit the needs of the schools more effectively. School technology team members, as school resource providers, often manage the specialized equipment, such as video cameras or microphones, and the training on collaborative software. Collaboration between schools, business, universities, and other schools require strong policies to protect the students, and the school technologists are the most appropriate people to assist in making collaborative decisions.

MANAGING COMMUNITY RESPONSE TO SCHOOL TECHNOLOGY POLICIES

While marketing and educating around school technology policies and procedures, many reactions occur. A decision to block Wikipedia.com throughout the district, for example, may be met by applause from the faculty, i.e., "It's not a real reference source, anyway!" and anger by students, i.e., "Why am I always blocked from the sites that make it easier to learn?" Managing the variety of responses from your community members is a challenge to say the least. Parents may get involved, questioning the role of district administrators who are making districtwide decisions for the protection of all students in the schools.

One of the biggest challenges in reactions with policies and procedures occurs because of misinformation. For example, teachers feel that the AUP implies that they are being watched every time their computers are used, students feel that all of the good Web sites are blocked, and parents feel that their children are missing out on fundamental education due to policy restrictions. Using the communication strategies from this chapter, many of these feelings can be dispelled because the policy development process encompasses more people and is more accommodating, not more restrictive.

Supportive Responses

Why manage supportive responses to instructional technology policies and procedures? First, you must clearly define what a supportive response looks like. Fewer policy-related infractions, survey results indicating more knowledgeable students and staff members on policies, and support by your district's legal counsel are all potential examples of positive feedback.

One of the values of positive feedback for technology policies and procedures is being able to identify where school technology policies are being implemented successfully. This allows you to investigate deeper to see if there are common threads of information that can lead you to more policies becoming part of a school culture. Another useful aspect of positive support is more global involvement in the development of new policies and procedures. Cultures that already support existing policies and procedures are great candidates for creating more realistic and useful policies in the future.

Negative Responses

On the other hand, some of your responses upon the implementation of policies and procedures may be negative. After all, negative feedback is at least reinforcement that your work has made an impact in the local schools. For example, your school or district may decide to block Google.com or Wikipedia.com to prevent inappropriate material from being displayed to students. Even if you have communicated the change, complaints may still be forwarded to you, especially if this changes access that students and teachers already have.

In my own case, when our school district blocked Wikipedia due to inappropriate content that could not be filtered out prior to displaying on students' machines. I received calls and e-mails (our filter has a link to click if you feel that a site is blocked inappropriately) from teachers, staff members, parents, and students. I even had one persistent student pose as a parent (who *just happened* to work as a lawyer in a New York law firm) to try to get the decision reversed. In this case, I simply reiterated the rationale and recommended the student use district-purchased research tools.

One of the best ways to deal with the negative responses is to continue focusing on the end goal: District technology is for teaching and learning and the support of teaching and learning. Educate your school community when major changes are coming, provide them with alternatives when possible, and ask your supporters to help you overcome negative emotions around changes. As mentioned, communication is the key, and strong communication pieces will need to be strategized carefully to ensure delivery to the right people or groups when changes are made. When negative responses to policies and procedures are expressed, you will have the right messages to deliver.

PREVENTING CONFLICTS OVER POLICY COMPONENTS

Since policy and procedure work often results in negative feedback, there are occasionally conflicts over the use of instructional technology. While there are a number of conflict resolution classes available, that is a whole different book. Resolving conflicts, whether those conflicts are about Web site use, computer availability, or technology requirements for classroom assignments, is part of the life of school technology leaders. For example, if you have computers in your school media centers, you may have parents who try to use the computers for personal work while school is in session and they are waiting for their child to be released for the day. Another challenge might arise when parents discover that their children's work is online and they tacitly signed a media release form when they received their children's student handbooks.

Regardless of the conflict, the importance of having a consistent strategy for conflict resolution is high. Consider implementing an appeal process so that school community members have a right to complain. This allows all sides to identify their perspectives and, if possible, create a path for resolution. Again, communication is a key instrument in your box of tools. Since conflicts arise when people's expectations are not fulfilled, e.g., "I expected you to take care of protecting my child from seeing inappropriate material" or "We expect our filtering solution to be appropriate for our students who are not misusing our technology," conflict resolution should be an exercise in clarifying expectations.

When working issues out around technology policies and procedures, a strong strategy is to first obtain agreement that students must be protected. Whether by law, e.g., CIPA and FERPA, or by school district policy or procedure, protecting students when using technology is essential. Second, school district resources must be used for the purposes of teaching and learning. Allowing others to discuss these two points first and then address resolving the conflict helps put the entire conversation into a more reasonable frame of mind.

SUMMARY

Well-designed policies support classroom activities and protect staff and students. While this may be a simplistic statement, the reality in many districts and schools is that policies are either overenforced to the point of making technology use difficult or neglected so that nobody knows what the real purpose or content of the policies are any more. The smartest way to implement policies is to constantly bring them into the "light" of the school, classroom, and district culture through structured communications and dedicated resources. If your school has one or more dedicated technology staff members, helping educate others on technology policies may be a useful component of their job descriptions. Finally, be prepared for both supportive and negative responses because there are typically both kinds of feedback when policies are implemented. Remember that culture changes take a great deal of time to implement, and a single meeting or discussion will not make lasting changes; it is the consistent, constant focus on protecting staff and students that will change the culture for significant periods of time.

One final note: George Bernard Shaw once wrote, "The danger in communication is the illusion that it has been accomplished." As with many of the topics in this chapter, effective communications provided by the school or district are the first critical step in changing the culture and building a systemic decisions that support appropriate technology use. Do not neglect this task, and do not ever assume that it is complete. It never will be.

REFERENCES

Campbell, N. (1998). *Writing effective policies and procedures a step-by-step resource for clear communication.* New York: American Management Association.

Deaney, R., & Hennessy, S. (2007). Sustainability, evolution, and dissemination of information and communication technology-supported classroom practice. *Research Papers in Education, 22*(1), 65–94.

Rosenfeld, B., & Martinez-Pons, M. (2005). Promoting classroom technology use. *The quarterly review of distance education, 6*(2), 145–153.

Stiler, G. M. (2005). MP3 players: Applications and implications for the use of popular technology in secondary schools. *Education, 128*(1), 20–33.

Woolsey, K., & Woolsey, M. (2008). Child's play. *Theory Into Practice, 47,* 128–137.

8

In My Crystal Ball, I See . . .

Emerging Technology Concerns

Critical Chapter Questions

- How can emerging technologies be used inappropriately?
- What emerging technologies can be used for instruction effectively?
- How can my school district protect students and staff from inappropriate technology use?

Chapter Focus: *Designing policies and procedures to meet the needs of emerging technologies.*

❖

Clarisse feels like she is running on a treadmill. Every week it seems there is a new piece of technology being brought into her school and there is yet another teacher demanding that it be installed in the classroom. As a member of the school technology team, she has worked to ensure that all teachers have a base level of technology and training in their classrooms, and the few "early adopter" technology-using teachers in her school have been very effective at spreading the word about the tools they use with students. Clarisse called the help desk several times but was told that the district help resources were only for "district approved" technology, not items purchased by the school or by teachers. While her principal's enthusiasm toward technology is supportive and encouraging for all of the staff members, the idea that technology will solve our teaching and learning problems has encouraged teachers to try everything under the sun in their classrooms. Even worse, there is no real substantive research being done to find out if the new technology has any impact on student learning. Unfortunately, the treadmill doesn't seem like it will slow down any time soon, and Clarisse is spending more and more time on repairing these odd pieces of hardware and software, and spending less time on staff development to help teachers use the district-supported teaching and learning applications.

POLICY CHALLENGES OF UBIQUITOUS TECHNOLOGY

If Clarisse's plight sounds somewhat like yours, you are not alone. From the principal to the classroom teacher, emerging technology has become a significant challenge in the classroom. The administrative challenges of emerging technologies are becoming massive headaches for schools and districts alike. Of course, device miniaturization is part of the challenge because greater technology capabilities can fit into a smaller and smaller package, escaping casual detection in the classroom. Consider, for example, the video camera. In addition to video cameras on phones and handheld audio devices, incredibly small, high-quality, and Web-ready cameras are about the size of a deck of playing cards and will only get smaller (for example, go to www.theflip.com).

As you might imagine, cell phones alone are a considerable worry for school administrators, and many school districts have created policies that dance around one of three positions on cell phones being used by students (Obringer & Coffey, 2007):

1. Students may not, under any circumstances, bring cell phones on campus.

2. Students may bring cell phones on campus, but they may not be visible or used during the school day.

3. Students do not have restrictions around cell phone use, as long as teaching and learning is not disrupted.

Among the concerns noted by researchers regarding cell phones, many are nonacademic, such as school environment disruptions, bullying activities, phoning in false bomb threats, and planning violent or illegal activities that include gang-related fighting and drug connections. Scholastically, cell phones can be used to cheat on assessments through text and media messaging, used as a calculator in math classes, and even as a maliciously intended video recorder of teacher activities.

Cell phones are just one of the challenges that district administrators face when crafting new policies and procedures. Managing emerging technology implies an ongoing awareness of what is being purchased at schools as well as what is being brought to schools by students and staff members. Whether the new technology is hardware, software, Internet related, or something in between, emerging technology is undefined, indefinable, and extremely difficult to predict. Policies slide out of date extremely quickly if they are not designed flexibly with room for growth and the intent of protecting teaching and learning activities.

Unethical Uses of School Technology

A key challenge in keeping policies "on the shelf" is the number of interesting, but nonacademic, uses of technology. Swapping files, taking pictures, updating profiles, watching videos, and sending e-mails could all be legitimate tasks, and many networks allow each of these activities. However, without a direct connection to teaching and learning, or support of teaching and learning, these specific uses of school technology can be highly suspicious and called into question. Unfortunately, many people, including staff and students, feel that the *access* to a resource means *approval* of the resource, which is certainly not the case.

As a result, many students and teachers use the network unethically. Many classes especially in middle and high school environments have periods of time with high levels of computer access, such as in computer labs. A teacher can only monitor so many students on computers at once, and many students see this as an opportunity to check personal e-mails, visit blogs or social networking sites (that have not been blocked yet), or use their cell phones to send messages to other students. Staff members spend hours surfing the Internet to the exclusion of teaching students or run businesses online while at schools.

Most states have several layers of legal statements that provide guidelines for use of public resources. There are typically state codes, court rulings, and codes of ethics for instructors to follow that make it clear that teachers are not to use publicly purchased technology for personal remunerative gain but the realistic connection between running an eBay store during planning periods is missing for a large number of teachers. If your school district issues cell phones to staff members at any level, are there guidelines or limits to the use of the device in addition to a monthly usage fee? How much personal information should be posted on teacher Web sites and can family photos of a teacher be uploaded to his or her Web page? All of these questions result from policies and procedures that cannot keep up with the changes in technology environments. Without the right emphasis on ethical technology uses in your school or district, there may be no final resolution at all.

Student-Owned Technology

Another main reason that technology policies expire so quickly in the teaching and learning fields is due to the clientele: students. With a higher level of access to technology and more time to research their preferences than many adults, students are constantly bringing new technology to school with them. Students may no longer experience an organized "show and tell" in the classroom, but they certainly share technological prowess on the recess field. At the younger grades, cell phones have become a status symbol. At the higher grades, students feel that bringing their personal laptops to school is a privilege reserved just for them. Whether the devices are MP3 players, cellular devices, tools that connect wireless to 3G networks, USB drives with applications on them, or a list of open-access proxy servers on them, many students are part of a highly technocratic caste system (Valadez & Duran, 2007).

When crafting policies to meet the needs of students bringing their own technology devices to schools, the local school administration and technology teams must be unified on how to address this eventuality. Technologically, how is the network locked down to prevent unauthorized usage, and is it appropriate (or feasible) to provide limited, filtered access for students with wireless devices? Ethically, what is the responsibility of the school or district to support these devices? Socially, how can the use of personally owned technology be discouraged in a school or district, and how will parents react? Policies can address each of these components, but the real questions should be, "How will this impact teaching and learning, and what risks are assumed by allowing students to bring their own technology to schools?"

Perhaps the most effective route is the "middle" perspective. Students and their parents sign a release form if the students absolutely must bring the computers to school but will have no access to school resources—no power, no online access, and no sharing of technology among students (Millard, 2005). As scholastic communities figure this particular challenge out, they will also need a strong process to inform their community and enforce the district's stance. If a student brings his own laptop, then plugs it into the school's power, is that a policy violation for your district? What are the consequences for not "checking in" any personal technology prior to use in a classroom?

The Perceived Right to Use School Technology

Along with emerging technology, there is also an emerging sense of entitlement to school technology resources by students, parents, and even the general public. Finding parents working on the school's media center computers, for example, has become a challenge that many schools have to face. Schools that have clearly defined policies about personal uses of technology in the school may still have to face this type of challenge because parents feel that technology in the schools is theirs to use when needed.

If your school is in a community-oriented environment, the school may be a "home" to churches, community schools, weekend enrichment classes, college classes, and even to sports events. Many of these groups using the schools also want some type of access to the school technology, either network access or (typically) computer access. For example, a baseball league involving many of the school's children wants to use a school computer lab to sign students up for the sports season. As a community outreach, the principal agrees to help the league by opening the lab for registration. Several questions arise: What user ID or password will be used? What applications or access will be provided? What kind of supervision will be given for students using the computers? What is the liability of the school district if the registration also includes online payments? Will acceptable use policies (AUPs) be required just to use the computers?

These types of questions are similar to those concerns raised when any new technology is introduced to the school. Access, acceptable use, and the value for teaching and learning must all be considered as quickly as possible for schools before the new technology is going to be brought to school, whether teachers or administrators like it or not. For instance, the parental defense that "my child needs to have a cell phone" is usually justified as being needed for safety reasons. What most parents miss, however, is that their children are much more likely to use cell phones to avoid teaching and learning tasks instead of keeping them "just for emergencies." However, as many principals will attest, parents hotly defend their children's "right" to keep cell phones at all times.

Creating policies to address these emerging challenges are not easy, especially since they must work within a mindset that the school is a community center not an environment for teaching and learning. Directing parents to the public library to use computers, for example, may not be comfortable to do but essential if your school or district intents to have computers available for teaching and learning at all times. Parents can also be informed throughout the year of the disruptions caused by cell phone use at schools along with helpful phone management tips that the school has gathered. Policies should continually and single-mindedly focus on the purposes of all school technology: teaching and learning or the support of teaching and learning. If the technology being brought into the school does not support these purpose, then the school has the right to enforce any restrictions necessary.

ADDRESSING EMERGING TECHNOLOGY AND LIMITING RISKS

Along with student-carried technology, technology for teaching and learning seems to arrive at schools by osmosis. Whether it is software that a teacher brought back from a conference, e.g., "Try it, this copy is free for you and your classroom!" or an organizational device being requested by an administrator, e.g., "I need to be able to check my e-mail when I am away from my desk!" or a hard drive plugged into a network computer for a classroom activity, e.g., "I need to show my students this clip from a movie that I downloaded!" there is often a great deal of emotion attached to new technology and its potential value to teaching and administration. Unfortunately, the correct amount of enthusiasm does not make the technology appropriate for your school's technology environment.

Only a few people are concerned about the risks of bringing emerging technology into a school: the technology team members and sometimes administrators. Teachers have a different focus, and, to be honest, probably should not have to worry about testing software for network compatibility. However, technology team members and administrators should be very aware of these concerns because a single application or piece of equipment has the potential to create havoc on the entire network. Even worse, students (and some staff members) who are not satisfied of their schools decide to act maliciously, which is a good reason for making policies, such as AUPs, actionable documents.

Connecting and Sharing With Others

As mentioned before in this text, the use of social networking sites is not going away any time soon and new multimedia capabilities will only reinforce the connections between people through technology. Risks emerge, however, in the development of school-centric social connections, such as blogs, video blogs—or vlogs, discussion boards, and even sites that mimic social networking sites for professional development or school communities (Yan, 2008). Teachers and schools are exploring the uses of text messaging, virtual "worlds," and video-based discussion forums for academic purposes. Connecting with others, though, has a price—who is monitoring these communications to protect the students and staff members from inappropriate technology use (Fleming, 2008)?

One of the key challenges on any network supporting interactive social networking is the need for bandwidth. Connecting with others has a very real cost in terms of the network's capabilities to support teaching and learning *and* allowing users to view or contribute streamed content. Without a thorough review process, emerging technology for collaboration may not fit the infrastructure needs of a school or district. In lieu of using streaming content, many schools and districts have begun to use blogs, wikis, and podcasts to create new ways for students to interact. As noted before, however, the these tools can be risky solutions to implement if the teacher is not prepared to monitor the entries vigilantly and there are policies to support disciplinary measures in the cases of inappropriate use (Hennessy, Deaney, & Ruthven, 2005).

For a purely technological challenge, consider the use of Bluetooth technology in school technology. Wireless tablets, keyboards, mice, and other computer input equipment have been manufactured using Bluetooth communications protocols and technology. With the advent of ubiquitous Bluetooth-enabled cell phones, these devices are not as accurate as they once were. Teachers using wireless input tablets to foster student interaction may have their tools go awry as students' cell phones interact with tablets, reception units, computers, overhead projectors, and the teachers' wireless keyboards and mice. Again, without a proper evaluation process, the end result may not be student learning but teacher frustration instead.

Policies to protect students and staff in the area of socially oriented technology should focus on the appropriate evaluation of tools for teaching and learning along with some clear guidelines on how the technology will enhance the classroom interaction. The evaluation of these learning plans is a first step in establishing the value of the new technology to the remainder of the staff or to other schools (Kirkley, 2004). Whether the technology will be adopted or not depends on its long-term applicability to the classroom, whether it makes teaching and learning more effective and whether or not the teacher feels competent in the use of the technology. While these may not be in the realm of policies, teachers and students should be aware of the appropriate manners in which technology can be used, which is part of a policy discussion.

Unethical Uses of Technology

Unlike teachers striving to use new technologies for teaching and learning, some students (and occasionally some teachers) choose to use school hardware, software, and resources for unethical uses. This is becoming more of a challenge as more students and staff members have wider access to technology resources. With high-speed wireless Internet networking available in coffee shops, bookstores, libraries, and restaurants, the ability to use school district technology to do things contrary to the AUP is becoming easier and easier. Now that many schools have issued laptops to teachers and students, the opportunity to install personal software, visit nonschool-related Web sites, and post inappropriate content on the Web through school technology has become more common.

Some of the challenges of addressing unethical use have grown since the Internet made media much more accessible to everyone. The term "free speech," once reserved for school discussions of student-written newsletters, has now ballooned into inappropriate use of school technology. Steven Baule and Darcy Kriha (2008) note,

> Many, if not most, adolescents utilize electronic social networking sites as a primary method of communicating and as a way of expressing themselves and displaying their thoughts, feelings, and ideas. Most of the time, social networking sites provide adolescents and young adults viable and healthy methods of self-expression. However, when those sites are used to propagate disruptive,

slanderous, or even threatening speech, educational environments are often impacted. (p. 22)

To create policies to handle these types of negative educational impacts, begin with filtering student access to sites where social networking does not have a scholastic value. Review the "free speech" policies in your district and include language to note that off-campus communications must not disrupt the school teaching and learning process. Be aware, though, that the courts have not clearly ruled in favor of schools or students; instead, the courts have been looking at the impact of non-scholastic activities to rule on whether or not student discipline is warranted. In addition to previous discussions, consider Layshock versus Hermitage SD, where a student MySpace page parodying the principal became a school sensation. The school did not filter MySpace at the time so the entire network had to be shut down, disrupting the educational process. Discipline was warranted because of the disruption, but if the page had not received such wide circulation, the ruling would probably have been different.

Unethical use of school or district technology can be viewed as vandalism. Anything that damages the quality of the learning process must be evaluated and prevented as well. Policies crafted with this concept in mind will generally be more tolerable to the courts than those that are not. Students are not the only perpetrators of such actions. In another example, one teacher videotaped an adjacent teacher for harassing or slanderous purposes. This clearly creates a hostile work environment and can be considered a cause for discipline. The fact that school technology was being used for this particular activity only added to the infraction and underscores the idea that teachers are not immune to unethical uses of technology.

Student-Managed Web Sites and Detrimental Pages

The latest iterations of self-publishing tools now includes streaming video, personalized pages, keyword indexing, graphic thumbnailing by metatags, and notification through subscription services. YouTube is just one example of this type of technology and there are more on the way. These tools are incredibly powerful and adaptable. Even when blocked at school, students with intelligent phones can play videos, upload videos and images, leave comments, and even craft entire Web pages just with a phone or Internet-capable handheld device such as an iPod Touch. Whether with a social networking site or not, students who use their posting-to-the-Web powers for evil—and *not* good—are certainly making situations more difficult for school administrators at every level.

Specialized applications have also arrived on the Internet "scene," designed to be a sort of black market of information. Consider two Web sites: www.ratemyprofessors.com and www.ratemyteachers.com. One of the growing demographics using these sites are parents who show up at open house nights and parent-teacher conferences with predetermined ideas about teacher quality and their children's educational needs. While these sites cannot be blocked by home computers, it is important that administrators and policy makers stay aware to ensure that they are blocked on district computers.

Next-Generation Social Networking Sites

The next generation of networking sites has been touted as both good and bad: *Good* because it will allow rapid connections among a wide group of people with the ability to share various media objects and artifacts of communication; *Bad* because networking sites can be developed and populated in a short period of time and difficult to track if malicious content is being posted. As an optimistic culture, educators are beginning to use social networking tools in the teaching and learning process. Whether it takes the form of virtual classes in virtual environments, class video logs and discussion groups, or team groups on education-only social networking tools, the need for multiple venues for student communication continues to be an area of need.

In order to use these sites for legitimate educational purposes, filtering will also need to be evaluated. Whether your district filters contextually through keywords or a combination of both, filters should address student-posted material for appropriateness prior to distributing. Content developed under a teacher's supervision can be made available through next generation social networking sites although most teachers do not understand the technical sides of posting material on the Web. However, more and more Web sites incorporate simple tools for network development, such as streamlined uploading tools or applications that collect pictures from a digital camera or phone.

One final note about social networking sites: Be aware. Social networking sites are not going away any time soon nor will it be possible to monitor every student posting or teacher Web site prior to broad distribution. However, what *can* be monitored is a set of policies, procedures, and guidelines for broad distribution to students and staff alike. A number of organizations can help you, so check with your local library organizations and with state and federal education offices for assistance. They may have resources that can be used or customized very quickly to help staff and students understand the impact of social networking in schools and school communities.

POLICY DEVELOPMENT TO SUPPORT FUTURE APPROPRIATE SCHOOL TECHNOLOGY USE

Creating instructional technology policies and procedures without fully understanding what is on the market is something like driving a car with no headlights at night. While you can see the general outlines of things you are approaching, you may not be able to see obstructions until a wreck is imminent. Preparing policies that are flexible and useful requires some patience because each district will have its own approach for the development and implementation of policies and procedures. Here are some key elements to consider when designing flexible policies and procedures:

- Avoid mentioning specific technologies, e.g., Facebook and iPod, and focus on the functionality of the technology, e.g., social networking or digital data device
- Keep the focus on teaching and learning or the support of teaching and learning
- Provide realistic examples in plain language to help readers understand the importance of their actions
- Clearly define the audience and their responsibilities for keeping students and staff safe
- Indicate the boundaries of authority, e.g., home use of district resources or personal video logs complaining about the school or district
- Identify consequences for unethical or inappropriate use

Educator Roles

Teachers, whether in classroom or administrative roles, often have excellent insight in the day-to-day impacts of technology in schools. When developing new policies and procedures, consider including several teachers on the development and review team. When teachers have students asking if their presentations can be taped as a video log or bring their homework assignments in to class saved on their music players or submit their homework using cell phones via e-mail, you know that they are brushing up against the up-and-coming technology.

Various grade levels will have their own challenges, however, so incorporate several groups into the policy development process. Try to find teachers or tech team members who are aware of, if not savvy about, the way their students are using technology. Are there Web sites, either blocked or unblocked, that are a major focus of student computer activity, and what can those Web sites tell you about the way technology use is changing? Can your teachers describe the technology that students bring into their classrooms? With that information, the policies and procedures can zero in on the important student technology and create reasonable guidelines for use.

Have teachers indicated that they need more technology training to keep up with the students in their classes? When teachers adopt new technology, they create a new "space" for students to share in the classroom about technologies in the students' lives (Hodge & Anderson, 2007). This new aptitude creates a unique knowledge point that is often missed by policy makers. Therefore, when you talk about instructional technology policies and procedures, remember to ask teachers what technology their students bring into the classroom *and* what technologies they would like to know more about. The teachers may not have vocalized their desire to keep up with their students' technology before, and you may find some interesting and unexpected results.

Administrator Roles

The key role of administrators when identifying new technology policy needs is when discipline comes into play. Strong administrators set a direction, create a culture, and, unfortunately, deal with the problems. As a result, administrators are an excellent source of information about the disruptions caused in classrooms by technology. They are also the face of contact with the parents and can help you understand how policies and procedures fit within the community framework of parents and community members (St. Gerard, 2006).

From the administrative perspective, policies either support their task at hand or get in the way of corrective actions, and principals certainly feel the pressure to enforce the rules or challenge rules that are not effective. Having principal input on policy development will also build a more collaborative team between policy makers and school administrators. With students bringing laptops to schools, cell phones being used during school hours to disrupt learning, and parents insisting that their children absolutely must have personal electronic devices on their persons at all times, administrators need strong policies to navigate among the viewpoints and factions that invariable arise.

Parental and Community Roles

Finally, parents and community members have a role in the development of instructional technology policies and procedures. Parents are definitely an asset to the policy development process because they have two unique perspectives: (1) the needs of technology-using students (2) along with the need for a solid education for their children. Parents' frustration about school policies is usually borne out of misunderstanding of policy or unclear consequences for students who violate the school rules. If the parent has to pick up the cell phone that their child was inappropriately using in class, the parent tends to voice his or her frustration with the school staff because they do not have the perspective of the entire school. With strong communication, these issues can be addressed, and while the parent may not be happy, he or she will at least understand the rules more thoroughly and know the consequences if the issue occurs a second time.

Community members can also bring insight to the policy-creation table because they too have a vested interest in students who graduate into a technology-rich workforce. Many work in companies where Internet use policies are more restrictive than school districts, and they can bring a fresh perspective to Web site blocking. Community members from the business sector can also provide examples and resources for communicating in the schools, such as policy templates, acceptable use guidelines, and filtering experience.

Parents and community members can also help evaluate and acquire instructional technology through sponsorships and fund drives. Emerging technology is sometimes very difficult for schools to acquire, so parent groups and community partners can play a role in finding new instructional technology and bringing resources to the table. If parents and community members are already part of the policy-making process, then they may also be excellent "researchers" for more powerful teaching tools. These school community members can also help define appropriate ways for teacher and students to use emerging technology in the classroom, such as business-to-school collaboration events or serving as guest speakers in career-focused discussion groups. With some creativity, parents and community members can be a powerful asset in developing policies for emerging technologies.

SUMMARY

If you have spent five minutes in the classroom or school environment, you know that technology is changing the way education is accomplished. A challenge arises, however, when technology "forms" change faster than policies, procedures, and school culture can accommodate. Whether the technology is student, staff, or district owned does not change the need to use technology in schools for teaching and learning and the support of teaching and learning. This includes software, online applications, and handheld devices, all of which are capable of amazing activities both for—and against—the school's primary mission of education. Policy development should focus on the roles in the school of educators, administrators, parents, and community members, and their responsibilities in teaching and learning. To increase flexibility in policies, avoid naming specific technology tools, such as iPod, Palm, BlackBerry, and focus instead on broader functions, such as audio, video, data, and communication tools. Finally, involve your school community in the development of policies and procedures because they will be able to inform your policy makers of the emerging technology opportunities . . . and challenges.

REFERENCES

Baule, S. M., & Kriha, D. L. (2008, February). Free speech in a MySpace world. *Library Media Connection, 22–24.*

Fleming, D. L. (2008). Youthful indiscretions: Should colleges protect social network users from themselves or others? *The New England Journal of Higher Education, 27–29.*

Hennessy, S., Deaney, R., & Ruthven, K. (2005). Emerging teacher strategies for mediating "technology-integrated instructional conversations": A sociocultural perspective. *The Curriculum Journal, 16*(3), 265–292.

Hodge, S., & Anderson, B. (2007). Teaching and learning with an interactive whiteboard: A teacher's journey. *Learning, Media, and Technology, 32*(3), 271–282.

Kirkley, S. (2004). Emerging technologies and learning environment design. *Techtrends, 49*(3), 2–3.

Millard, E. (2005). Unplugged but locked down: Colleges and universities have worked to boost their wireless might—without causing security risks. *University Business, 8*(10) 41–44.

Obringer, S., & Coffey, K. (2007). Cell phones in American high schools: A national survey. *Journal of Technology Studies, 33*(1), 41–47.

St. Gerard, V. (2006). Updating policy on the latest risks for students with cell phones in the school. *Education Digest, 72*(4), 43–45.

Valadez, J. R., & Duran, R. (2007, February). Redefining the digital divide: Beyond access to computers and the Internet. *The High School Journal, 31–44.*

Yan, J. (2008). Social technology as a new medium in the classroom. *The New England Journal of Higher Education, 22*(4) 27–30.

Resources

Priming the Digital Pump:
Sample Documents and Templates

T he following resources are provided as starting or discussion points for district technology policies and procedures. They are not meant to be definitive but illustrative and may not fit within your school culture. Make sure to look online since many school districts have their policies and procedures online for review and are willing to share their policy development with other school districts. Groups such as the National School Board Association, regionally based technology support groups, and international associations (ISTE, CoSN) all are excellent places to start looking for specific information.

SAMPLE ACCEPTABLE USE POLICY COMPONENTS

As noted in Chapter 5, *Knowing the Secret Handshake: Technology Access Policies,* a number of components can be included in acceptable use policies (AUPs). Each of these sections should be written with the district or school's own voice.

- Computing facilities will be used exclusively for educational purposes. A review of the school or district's perception of what technology really is for that district should be included in this section.
- Students and teachers will use educationally appropriate speech and expression when using the Internet, which avoids profanity, unprofessional behavior, and inappropriate discussions, but promotes improved communication skills.
- Users are responsible for avoiding copyright violations (implying that your district has copyright policies already in place). For more information on this topic, go to the American Library Association (www.ala.org).
- Users have a reasonable expectation of privacy, which should be defined, at least in internal documents. If your school or district retain the right to perform technology use audits, this should be explained (random audits, only when there are disciplinary actions pending, or on regular, ongoing basis) and then communicated periodically to the users.
- User's responsibilities to avoid substantial and material disruption of the educational process for the school community. This statement should be included to protect the teaching and learning activities at the school.
- Consequences for inappropriate use should also be explained.
- For staff members and technology team members, consider the following components as well:

  o Professionally derived data and information will be protected and maintained in accordance with Family Educational Rights and Privacy Act (FERPA) guidelines. This should indicate additional documents, if necessary, that are part of the school or district's FERPA protection measures.
  o Staff use of technology will conform to ethical guidelines set forth by the state's standards commission. Ethical compliance is usually included in annual mandatory training sessions, as well as in certification renewal activities.
  o Users' responsibilities to protect and maintain others' resources through appropriate safety and security measures. If a user is a technology team member, he or she will have additional access that must be used ethically and appropriately.

SAMPLE INFORMATION ACCESS POLICY COMPONENTS

Information access, simply defined, means who can access what data resources using school technology. This may sound overwhelming, but the policy should be developed with an eye on the intent for providing students and staff with the information they need to perform their tasks.

- Access availability should be defined in terms of applications. What major systems are in place, such as human resources, finance, student information, and email, and which ones have security in place around them? What information is for public disclosure (school Web pages), need-to-know disclosure (student grades, assessment data), or employee-only disclosure (employee benefits information)?
- Data access must be protected by passwords and appropriate security measures. How does your school or district protect data resources? Clear definitions need to be made of administrative rights to data, which is different than student rights, or staff member rights to information collected by the school or district.
- Customer service structures should be included in the policy, indicated the types of assistance available to staff members when they request help with hardware, software, or Internet application issues.
- Consider including e-mail, e-mail archiving, and e-mail disclosure as a separate section in your policies and procedures. As noted in several chapters, e-mail can quickly become a source of data risk for the district or school.
- Protecting usernames, passwords, and other sensitive data should be part of the policy and procedure information as well. Guidelines for developing and protecting strong passwords can be included in this section, too.

SAMPLE INTERNET POLICY COMPONENTS

Internet use and development policies can be complex or simple, and it depends on your district's philosophy on Internet use. Many of the specific examples below are consistent with policies and procedures in districts throughout the country, and should be modified to fit your district or school needs. The following bullets are ideas to consider when crafting or reviewing your existing policies and procedures:

- Define the Internet as a tool for teaching and learning and the support of teaching and learning is essential.
- Define public information that is available on each school's Web site within the district. Many schools have guidelines in place to cover Web sites, but many schools place inconsistent levels and amounts of information on their Web pages within a typical district. See below for more ideas regarding Web site development.
- Identify areas of sensitive information. What information, such as instructional application login information, should be kept private? If your district has an online campus or subscribes to services requiring login information then defining sensitive information is important. As always, usernames and passwords are considered sensitive but remember to include student names, parent names, and media depicting students as well. What are your school or district's guidelines around taping public performances? Part of your Internet-facing policies might need to include a short discussion of media release forms as well.
- Clarify the use of parent-, student-, and staff-facing portals by defining the access available to each, along with the security measures in place to protect the identity and use of sensitive information. Student grades, attendance, e-mail, free- and reduced-lunch status, and course transcripts are just a few of the components of many portals, and your district may want to consider crafting policy statements around the data that is viewable in the portals.
- Refer to the AUPs in your school or district to ensure compliance for using the Web and other technology resources for teaching and learning.
- Include consequences for inappropriate use of the Internet. While policies should probably begin with the more positive uses of technology, consequences for inappropriate or unprofessional use of district technology may need to be clarified, including any state or federal law components appropriate for the area of acceptable use.

SAMPLE TECHNOLOGY INVESTMENT PROTECTION GUIDELINES

Statement by the School Board Regarding Use of Technology

The board supports the safe, effective use of technology for teaching and learning and support of teaching and learning. Technology shall be used in support of our district's vision, mission, and goals, and uphold the ethical responsibilities of staff members and students. The board also recognizes that electronic media, including the Internet, provides access to a wide variety of instructional resources in an effort to enhance educational opportunities. Use of electronic resources must be in support of, and consistent with the vision, mission, and goals established by the board and for the purpose of instructional support. All users of the districtwide area network and other electronic information resources must maintain compliance with all applicable ethical and legal rules and regulations regarding access.

Anticipated Uses of Technology in the Classroom

Network users are individually responsible for following local, state, national, and international copyright, intellectual property rights, and adhering to acceptable network use.

Option 1: All use of the system must be in support of education and research and consistent with the mission of the district. District reserves the right to prioritize use and access to the system. Any use of the system must be in conformity to state and federal laws, K–20 network policies, and district policies.

Option 2: School district technology should be used for legitimate educational reasons only and not for personal use. Access is a privilege, not a right, and all students are expected to treat this learning tool with respect.

Option 3: By providing network access, the school district intends only to provide a means for educational activities and does not intend to create a first amendment forum for free expression purposes. The district dedicates the property comprising the network and grants access to it by users only for the educational activities authorized under this policy and procedures and under the specific limitations contained therein.

Inappropriate Uses of Technology

Learners using the district network should be aware that it is impossible to control, predict, and filter all materials a user may discover using district technology. In compliance with federal laws, our district will provide education on the proper use of electronic media, including the Internet. Neither the school district, nor any district staff member, controls all of the content available on these other systems. Some of the

(Continued)

(Continued)

information available is controversial and sometimes may be offensive. The school district *does not condone* the use of such materials. Therefore, it is imperative that the user be held accountable for the appropriate utilization of this technology.

- Harming others through technology use
- Performing illegal activities through technology use
- Gaining unauthorized access to other people's files, data, e-mail, or programs
- Gaining unauthorized access through the use of someone else's username and password
- Improperly using the network, including the introduction of software viruses or unauthorized software
- Bypassing local school or school district security measures
- Damaging the technology network
- Access upload, download, and distribute pornographic, hate-oriented, profane, obscene, or sexually explicit material
- Using technology to cheat or steal instructional materials
- Using the system for commercial solicitation is prohibited

Consequences of Inappropriate Uses of Technology

Access is a privilege—not a right! Inappropriate use will result in a cancellation of these privileges as well as possible assignment of disciplinary action consistent with the policies and procedures of the school district.

Local schools may establish additional regulatory guidelines for use of electronic resources that include, but are not limited to, guidelines established by this systemwide procedure. Building administrators shall establish a process for informing students and staff about the district and local school AUPs.

- **Where to find more information** For more information, please contact <district contact here>.
- **Signature lines** I have read and understand <School District>'s AUP and I will abide by these guidelines. I further understand that violation of these guidelines may result in the loss of access privileges and that school discipline and legal action may be taken.

Student Signature and Date

Option 1: As the parent or guardian of this student, I have read this information and understand that student technology resources are intended for educational purposes. I understand that it is impossible for <the school district> to restrict access to all controversial materials, and I will not hold the district or <the local school> responsible for materials acquired on the network. I also agree to report any misuse of the information systems of which I become aware to the appropriate district authorities. Misuse may take many forms but can be viewed as any network use that indicates or suggests pornography, unethical, or illegal solicitation, racism, sexism, inappropriate language, and other issues described above.

Option 2: I hereby give my permission for my child to use the wide range of electronic services available to her or him while attending a district school I hereby release the school district, its operators, and any institutions with which they are affiliated from any and all claims and damages of any nature arising from my child's use of, or inability to use, the system, including, without limitation, the types of damage identified in the school district's policy and administrative regulations.

Parent Signature and Date

- **<Optional> Password Maintenance and Privacy** As a school district employee, volunteer, or vendor, you will be expected to maintain appropriate passwords to obtain access for your job or tasks. All district-issued passwords should be changed within one week of issuance by the user if the application enables the user to do so. Not all applications allow this, but the applications where the password should be changed immediately include <list applications>. Passwords should be changed every 90 days thereafter to maintain the integrity of the network.
- **<Optional> Clarification of Administrative Rights** Example 1: Technology team members may not access electronic resources without proper authorization by their supervisor and by <authority-granting group within the district>.

  o Example 2: Technology team members have access to administer technology at their school or district for the purpose of performing specific job roles given to them by their supervisors. Use of administrative access outside of their specific job roles shall be considered an inappropriate use of technology within the school or school district.

- **<Optional> Final Authority on Disputes** Please note that school district technology use is subject to auditing for legitimate purposes as well as live monitoring where appropriate. The <appropriate school division> has been given the charge to perform network monitoring to include specific investigations. If a technology team member feels that such an investigation should occur, he or she needs to contact his or her supervising administrator and then the supervising administrator should contact the superintendent <and the chief information officer>.
- **<Optional> Student Data Protection.** At no time should student names be broadcast or disclosed in unauthorized communications sent outside the school district network. For example, a teacher-initiated progress report sent through e-mail to a parent is appropriate, but posting individually identifiable student testing data on a nondistrict Web site is not appropriate. Teachers should closely monitor classroom activities where students are communicating to others

(Continued)

(Continued)

outside of the district. Such activities might be classroom-to-classroom collaborative projects, "pen pals" and Web site–related instructional activities. At no time should student privacy be compromised in these communications, nor should students' work be delivered outside of the school district without direct supervision of the students' teacher. Student and staff data may be transmitted periodically to educational and government entities for required business purposes, but these transmissions are managed in a secure environment to maintain student and staff confidentiality.

- **<Optional> Modeling Appropriate Technology Use Behavior** Staff members, vendors, and volunteers using district technology are responsible for protecting their own network accounts and are solely responsible for all actions taken while accessing and using information resources. The user will work in a moral and ethical fashion that supports district educational goals. Certified staff members are also obligated to follow ethics guidelines provided by <state ethics guidelines information>.
- **<Optional> References to Other Policies and Procedures Concerning Ethical Behavior** For more information, please see the following policies and procedures: <List of policies and procedures, as well as access information for these documents.>

Sources for Additional Information

- A review of the potential legal challenges to the application of the Children's Internet Protection Act (CIPA) in public libraries [and schools]: Strategies and Issues. Paul T. Jaeger and Charles R. McClure.http:// www.firstmonday.org/ issues/issue 9_2/ jaeger/
- Joint Statement Opposing Legislative Requirements for School and Library Internet Blocking Technologies, by the Electronic Frontier Foundation. http://www.eff.org/Censorship/Censorware/20010117_joint_censorware_state ment.html
- From Now On—*Educational Technology Journal*, *5*(5) March-April 1996, A Dozen Reasons Why Schools Should Avoid Filtering. (Note: Very interesting perspectives since there will be some people within the school population who will agree with some or all of these points. It's good to know your opposition!) http://fromnowon.org/mar96/whynot.html
- A district's guide to assist K–12 school districts and other K–12 entities in developing their own acceptable use policy. http:// www.k12.wa.us/ K—20/AUP.aspx

Sample Technology Investment Protection Guidelines

Protecting school district technology often requires a review of different damage incidents that have already occurred and trying to divine what the next types of technology damage will be. Many school districts are willing to share their expertise on making policies to protect technology investments but your school or district many need to craft an interim policy to address pressing needs.

- Laptop use and protection is a core topic, including defining laptop recipients in a school and their responsibilities toward that equipment. For example, if a laptop is stolen, who is responsible? Topics to include in this policy include software loading, off-campus technology liability, and regular maintenance.
- Technology repair is a broad topic that needs to be defined, along with concepts such as negligence, line-of-duty damage, and methods for requesting repair assistance. If the cost of repairs is going to be distributed among staff members or schools depending on the type of repair, such as a teacher accidentally dropped a cup of coffee into a laptop keyboard, then your human resources department needs to be part of the policy-development discussion.
- Standard technology equipment is another topic to include in policies and procedures especially if your school's upgrade efforts are designed to standardize the types of technology available for teaching and learning. This is also a valuable policy if your school has received donations of equipment that require frequent upgrading or repair even though it is not standard equipment and costs more to repair. Defining the "classroom package" of technology and the guidelines around purchasing standard, supportable equipment in the schools or offices is a useful management resource.

SCHOOL WEB PAGE COMPONENTS

An interesting study of the components of school Web sites was chronicled by Miller, Adsit, and Miller (2005) in "Evaluating the Importance of Common Components in School-Based Web Sites: Frequency of Appearance and Stakeholders' Judged Value." They evaluated a variety of Web site contents and then surveyed parents to identify the most important components of the school Web sites as well. Certainly worth reading, and perhaps replicating, if your school or district does not have a standard established yet. The Web site components are

- Mission statement
- Rules and policies
- Curriculum and standards
- Teacher information
- Home school organization information
- Grade-level information pages
- Classroom-level information pages
- School news
- Homework hotline
- Breakfast and lunch menus
- School calendar
- Links for teachers, parents, and students
- Student work samples
- Physical location of school
- Internet use policy

REFERENCES

Conn, K. (2002). *The Internet and the law: What educators need to know.* Alexandria, VA: *ASCD.*

Miller, S., Adsit, K. I., & Miller, T. (2005). Evaluating the importance of common components in school-based Web sites: Frequency of appearance and stakeholders' judged value. *TechTrends: Linking Research and Practice to Improving Learning, 49*(6), 34–40.

Index

CORWIN

A SAGE Company

The Corwin logo—a raven striding across an open book—represents the union of courage and learning. Corwin is committed to improving education for all learners by publishing books and other professional development resources for those serving the field of PreK–12 education. By providing practical, hands-on materials, Corwin continues to carry out the promise of its motto: **"Helping Educators Do Their Work Better."**

AMERICAN ASSOCIATION
OF SCHOOL ADMINISTRATORS

The American Association of School Administrators, founded in 1865, is the professional organization for more than 13,000 educational leaders across the United States. AASA's mission is to support and develop effective school system leaders who are dedicated to the highest quality public education for all children. For more information, visit www.aasa.org.

NATIONAL ASSOCIATION OF SECONDARY SCHOOL PRINCIPALS

promoting excellence in middle and high school leadership

In existence since 1916, the National Association of Secondary School Principals (NASSP) is the preeminent organization of and national voice for middle level and high school principals, assistant principals, and aspiring school leaders from across the United States and more than 45 countries around the world. The mission of NASSP is to promote excellence in middle and high school leadership. NASSP administers the National Honor Society®, National Junior Honor Society®, National Elementary Honor Society®, and National Association of Student Councils®. For more information about NASSP, located in Reston, VA, visit www .principals.org.

DATE DUE